What Are...
Medicare Appeals?

SECOND EDITION

JESSICA L. GUSTAFSON
ABBY PENDLETON

AMERICAN**BAR**ASSOCIATION

Health Law Section

Cover design by Mary Ann Kulchawik/ABA Design.
Interior design by Betsy Kulak/ABA Design.

Printed in the United States of America.

25 24 23 22 21   5 4 3 2 1

ISBN: 978-1-64105-907-7

Discounts are available for books ordered in bulk. Special consideration is given to state bars, CLE programs, and other bar-related organizations. Inquire at Book Publishing, ABA Publishing, American Bar Association, 321 N. Clark Street, Chicago, Illinois 60654-7598.

www.shopABA.org

Contents

Introduction

The Medicare program is the second-largest social insurance program in the United States, second only to the Social Security Program. With more than 60 million beneficiaries,[1] the Centers for Medicare & Medicaid Services (CMS) processes more than 1 billion Medicare Part A and Part B Fee-for-Service (FFS) claims each year,[2] with total expenditures of more than $410 billion.[3] The vast majority (i.e., approximately 99.7 percent) of these claims are processed without undergoing claims review,[4] creating vulnerability for the Medicare Trust Funds. In 2020, an estimated $25.74 billion in improper payments were made.[5] Authorized by various legislative actions, CMS has contracted with entities to perform post-payment and pre-payment claims review aimed to measure, identify, prevent, correct, and stop improper payments. Health care provid-

---

1. http://www.cms.gov/Research-Statistics-Data-and-Systems/Statistics-Trends-and-Reports/ReportsTrustFunds/index.html?redirect=/ReportsTrust Funds.
2. Annual Report to Congress, Medicare and Medicaid Integrity Programs, FY 2018 at p. 5, *available at* https://www.cms.gov/files/document/medicare-and-medicaid-integrity-program-fy-2018-annual-report.pdf.
3. *See* Annual Improper Payments Datasets, Payment Accuracy 2020 Dataset, *available at* https://www.paymentaccuracy.gov/payment-accuracy-the-numbers.
4. Center for Program Integrity, Request for Information issued October 21, 2019, *available at* https://www.klgates.com/CMS-Requests-Information-on-Using-Advanced-Technology-in-Program-Integrity-11-05-2019.
5. CMS Fact Sheet: 2020 Estimated Improper Payment Rates for Medicare & Medicaid Services (CMS) Programs, *available at* https://www.cms.gov/newsroom/fact-sheets/2020-estimated-improper-payment-rates-centers-medicare-medicaid-services-cms-programs#:~:text=The%20FY%202020%20Medicare%20FFS,%2428.91%20billion%20in%20improper%20payments..

ers and suppliers that have received a Medicare FFS claim denial or overpayment determination may appeal the initial determination through a five-stage uniform Part A and Part B appeals process.

This book provides an overview of the Medicare FFS audit and Medicare appeals environment. Chapter 1 presents an overview of the various CMS contractors performing claims review (including post-payment and pre-payment auditing activities). Chapter 2 describes the uniform Medicare Part A and Part B appeals process. Chapter 3 sets forth appeal strategies and legal challenges applicable to Part A and Part B unfavorable claims determinations, with which attorneys should familiarize themselves when representing a health care entity subject to audit. A list of resources and references is included at the conclusion of this book.

About the Authors

Jessica L. Gustafson is a founding shareholder of The Health Law Partners, P.C. Admitted to the bars of both Michigan and New York, she practices in the firm's Farmington Hills, Michigan, headquarters. She devotes a substantial portion of her practice to representing providers and suppliers in the Medicare, Medicaid and other payor audit appeals processes. She also regularly assists clients with compliance and reimbursement matters, issues surrounding Medicare enrollment, and other health care regulatory matters. Representative clients include hospitals and health systems, physicians, hospices, home health agencies, and other health care providers and suppliers.

Ms. Gustafson is a frequent speaker to legal and health care provider and supplier audiences nationwide. She is also a frequent contributor and author to various health care and health law publications. She currently serves as the Co-Chair of the American Bar Association Health Law Section Membership Committee and a Vice Chair of its newsletter publication, *ABA Health eSource.*

Abby Pendleton is a founding shareholder of The Health Law Partners, P.C. Admitted to the bars of both Michigan and New York, Ms. Pendleton practices in the firm's Farmington Hills, Michigan, headquarters as well as in its New York location.

Ms. Pendleton has been practicing health care law since 1996. She regularly provides counsel to health care providers, suppliers, and organizations in a number of areas, including but not limited to government investigations; fraud and abuse; compliance; reimbursement; payor audits; HIPAA; and physician staff privilege and licensing matters. Ms. Pendleton also specializes in legal issues impacting billing and management companies, anesthesia and pain management providers, hospice providers, and mental health agencies.

Ms. Pendleton is a frequent speaker and author on a multitude of health care legal topics.

Chapter 1

Medicare Part A and Part B Audits

The Centers for Medicare & Medicaid Services (CMS) has adopted and implemented numerous Medicare auditing initiatives, each with slightly different goals:

- Comprehensive Error Rate Testing (CERT) audits *measure* improper payments in the Medicare Fee-for-Service (FFS) program;[1]
- Medicare Administrative Contractor (MAC) audits are designed to *prevent* improper payments through evaluation of program vulnerabilities and taking necessary action;[2]
- Supplemental Medical Review Contractor (SMRC) audits also are intended to *prevent* improper payments through evaluation of program vulnerabilities and taking necessary action;[3]

---

1. *See* MEDICARE PROGRAM INTEGRITY MANUAL (MPIM) (CMS Pub. 100-08) [hereinafter MPIM], Ch. 1, section 1.3.2, *available at* https://www.cms.gov/ Regulations-and-Guidance/Guidance/Manuals/Internet-Only-Manuals-IOMs-Items/CMS019033.
2. *Id.*
3. *Id.*

- Recovery Audits, formerly known as Recovery Audit Contractor (RAC) audits, are for the purpose of identifying and *correcting* improper payments;[4] and
- Unified Program Integrity Contractor (UPIC) audits are intended to *identify* and *stop* incidences of fraud in the Medicare program.[5]

The CMS Center for Program Integrity (CPI) oversees the Medicare medical review contractors.[6]

Although audits conducted by each of the above-listed contractors involves similar processes, there are slightly different requirements for each contractor. This chapter describes each of these contractors and provides an overview of the audit processes for each.

A. Comprehensive Error Rate Testing (CERT) Audits

The Payment Integrity Information Act of 2019 (PIIA)[7] requires the director of the Office of Management and Budget (OMB) to:

- Identify a list of high-priority federal programs for greater levels of oversight and review due to a high rate of or risk for improper payments;
- Estimate the amount of improper payments within those high-priority federal programs and submit such estimates to Congress; and

---

4. *Id.*
5. *See* MPIM *supra* note 1, Ch.1, section 1.7.
6. https://www.cms.gov/Research-Statistics-Data-and-Systems/Monitoring-Programs/Medicare-FFS-Compliance-Programs/Medical-Review.
7. *See* 31 U.S.C. § 3352 (b) and (c).

- Report to the public actions the agency has taken or plans to take to recover improper payments and intends to take to prevent future improper payments.[8]

The purpose of the CERT program is to measure and estimate improper payments in the Medicare FFS program[9] in compliance with the PIIA. "Improper payments" are defined to include both overpayments and underpayments.[10]

The Medicare FFS improper payment rate was first measured in 1996. Based on a sample size of just 6,000 claims annually, from 1996 to 2002, the Department of Health and Human Services (HHS) Office of Inspector General (OIG) estimated the national Medicare FFS paid claims error rate.[11] Due to the small sample size, the OIG produced only a national Medicare FFS paid claims error rate; the OIG did not estimate contractor-level error rates, service-specific error rates, or provider-type error rates.[12]

Building on the OIG's methodology, CMS established the CERT program and took over responsibility for measuring and estimating the Medicare FFS error rate beginning in 2003.[13] The sample size audited by CERT review contractors is much larger than was his-

---

8. 31 U.S.C. § 3352. Medicare FFS has been identified as high risk for improper payments. *See, e.g.*, U.S. GAO, Medicare Payment, Management, and Program Integrity, available at http://www.gao.gov/key_issues/medicare_payment_management _integrity/issue_summary.

9 MPIM, *supra* note 1, Ch. 1, section 1.3.1.

10. 31 U.S.C. § 3351(4).

11. http://www.cms.gov/Research-Statistics-Data-and-Systems/Monitoring-Programs/Medicare-FFS-Compliance-Programs/CERT/Background.html.

12. *See, e.g.,* IMPROPER FISCAL YEAR 2002 MEDICARE FEE-FOR-SERVICE PAYMENTS, A-17-02-02202 (January 2003), *available at* https://oig.hhs.gov/oas/reports/ cms/170202202.pdf.

13. *See* IMPROPER MEDICARE FEE-for-SERVICE PAYMENTS FISCAL YEAR 2003 (December 9, 2003), *available at* http://www.cms.gov/Research-Statistics-Data-and-Systems/Monitoring-Programs/Medicare-FFS-Compliance-Programs/ CERT/Downloads/FY2003LongReport.pdf.

torically audited by the OIG (i.e., approximately 50,000 claims).[14] Accordingly, the CERT program is able to measure and estimate not only a national FFS paid claims error rate but also a contractor-level error rate, service-specific error rate, and error rate by provider type.[15] This error rate information is used to inform the priorities of the other Medicare audit contractors.

The Medicare FFS error rate measurement and estimation process begins when the CERT statistical contractor[16] creates a universe file from claims entered into Medicare's claims processing system. Next, a random sample of claims is selected from the universe file for inclusion in the CERT sample.[17] After a specified period of time has elapsed to ensure processing of the claims, the CERT review contractor and the MACs exchange detailed information regarding the sampled claims, including the claims' resolution files; the claims' history replica files; and the providers' addresses.[18]

The CERT review contractor uses the information received from the MACs to request documentation from providers and suppliers

---

14. *See* http://www.cms.gov/Research-Statistics-Data-and-Systems/Monitoring-Programs/Medicare-FFS-Compliance-Programs/CERT/Background.html.

15. *See, e.g.,* CERT REPORTS, *available at* http://www.cms.gov/Research-Statistics-Data-and-Systems/Monitoring-Programs/Medicare-FFS-Compliance-Programs/CERT/CERT-Reports.html.

16. The CERT contractors include: (1) CERT Review Contractor and (2) CERT Statistical Contractor. *See* CERT Information for Providers, *available at* https://www.cms.gov/Research-Statistics-Data-and-Systems/Monitoring-Programs/Medicare-FFS-Compliance-Programs/CERT/InformationforProviders.

17. *See* MPIM, *supra* note 1, Ch. 1, section 1.3.5, and Ch. 12, section 12.3; and http://www.cms.gov/Research-Statistics-Data-and-Systems/Monitoring-Programs/Medicare-FFS-Compliance-Programs/CERT/Background.html. The sample is taken by claim type: Part A (excluding acute inpatient hospital services), Part A (only acute inpatient hospital services), Part B, and DME. *See generally* CERT REPORTS, http://www.cms.gov/Research-Statistics-Data-and-Systems/Monitoring-Programs/Medicare-FFS-Compliance-Programs/CERT/CERT-Reports.html.

18. MPIM, *supra* note 1, Ch. 12, section 12.3.

to support the sampled claims.[19] Requested documentation must be submitted by the date specified on the CERT review contractor's request for documentation.[20] The CERT review contractor will review the documentation and determine whether the claims were paid properly under Medicare coverage, coding, and billing rules.[21] The CERT review contractor utilizes licensed registered nurses (RNs), therapists, and physicians in reviewing claims; the CERT review contractor is "encouraged," but not mandated, to use certified coders to determine the correct coding for reviewed claims.[22] If Medicare criteria are not met or if requested medical records are not submitted within 75 days,[23] an error may be assigned to a claim, and an improper payment category will be assigned (i.e., no documentation, insufficient documentation, medical necessity, incorrect coding, or other errors).[24]

Of particular significance for health care providers and suppliers undergoing medical review performed by a CERT contractor, CMS has been clear that the purpose of CERT audits is not to identify fraudulent claims.[25] The sample of claims reviewed per

---

19. *Id.*

20. *See* MPIM *supra* note 1, Ch. 3, section 3.2.3.2. The CERT contractor has authority to provide extensions to this time frame.

21. https://www.cms.gov/Research-Statistics-Data-and-Systems/ Monitoring-Programs/Medicare-FFS-Compliance-Programs/CERT/ Background.

22. *See* MPIM, *supra* note 1, Ch. 3, section 3.3.1.1. Licensed practical nurses (LPNs) who currently work for the CERT contractor are "grandfathered in" and may perform medical reviews; however, the CERT contractor may not hire new LPNs to perform medical reviews. *Id.*

23. MPIM, *supra* note 1, Ch. 12, section 12.3.9.

24. *See, e.g.,* CERT REPORTS, *available at* http://www.cms.gov/Research-Statistics -Data-and-Systems/Monitoring-Programs/Medicare-FFS-Compliance- Programs/CERT/CERT-Reports.html.

25. *Id.*

provider or supplier is simply too small to identify patterns that may suggest fraud and abuse.[26]

The final step in the CERT audit process is for the CERT contractors to compile the data collected to estimate the national FFS claims paid error rate, contractor-level error rate, service-specific error rate, and provider-type error rate.[27]

When the CERT review contractor identifies an improper payment, the CERT review contractor notifies the applicable MAC, which adjusts the claim.[28] A health care provider or supplier that has received notice of a CERT review contractor's finding of improper payment may appeal this determination through the standard five-stage uniform Part A and Part B appeals process outlined in Chapter 2. Appeals of CERT determinations are required to be expedited, so that data can be corrected and finalized for inclusion in error rate reporting.[29]

B. Medicare Administrative Contractor (MAC) Audits

When the Medicare program was established in 1965, two types of contractors were used to administer the program: fiscal intermediaries (with responsibility for Part A claims) and carriers (with responsibility for Part B claims).[30] Section 911 of the Medicare

---

26. The per-provider sample size is generally less than 300 claims. *See, e.g.,* Comprehensive Error Rate Testing (CERT) Program (June 15, 2010) [hereinafter CERT Program], *available at* http://www.cms.gov/Research-Statistics-Data-and-Systems /Monitoring-Programs/CERT/downloads/CERT_Ed.pdf. *See also* HHS OIG, "CMS and Its Contractors Did Not Use Comprehensive Error Rate Testing Program Data to Identify and Focus on Error-Prone Providers," A-05-17-00023, January 2021, available at https://oig.hhs.gov/oas/reports/region5/51700023.pdf.
27. *See* http://www.cms.gov/Research-Statistics-Data-and-Systems/Monitoring -Programs/Medicare-FFS-Compliance-Programs/CERT/Background.html.
28. MPIM, *supra* note 1, Ch. 12, section 12.3.4.
29. *See id.* at section 12.3.6.1.
30. *See generally* Title XVIII of the Social Security Act, 42 U.S.C. § 1395 (July 30, 1965).

Prescription Drug, Improvement and Modernization Act of 2003 (MMA; Pub. L. No. 108–173) required CMS to replace fiscal intermediaries and carriers with MACs.[31] Through competitively procured contracts, the MACs were awarded specific geographic jurisdictions to process Medicare Part A and Part B claims or Durable Medical Equipment (DME) claims.[32] There are currently 16 MAC jurisdictions (comprised of 12 MAC jurisdictions for processing Part A and Part B claims and four DME MAC jurisdictions for processing DME claims).[33]

Specific tasks for which MACs have responsibility extend beyond audits of health care claims. The MACs' responsibilities include, but are not limited to, the following:

- Process Medicare FFS claims
- Enroll providers and suppliers into the Medicare FFS program
- Establish Local Coverage Determinations (LCDs)
- Educate providers and suppliers about Medicare billing requirements
- Audit institutional provider cost reports
- Review medical records for selected claims
- Process and respond to requests for redetermination (the first stage in the Medicare FFS appeals process, addressed in detail in Chapter 2)[34]

MACs are authorized to perform medical review of any and all claims submitted to them;[35] however, MACs focus medi-

---

31. https://www.cms.gov/Medicare/Medicare-Contracting/Medicare-Administrative-Contractors/What-is-a-MAC.
32. *Id.*
33. https://www.cms.gov/Medicare/Medicare-Contracting/Medicare-Administrative-Contractors/Who-are-the-MACs. *See also* 42 C.F.R. § 421.400.
34. https://www.cms.gov/Medicare/Medicare-Contracting/Medicare-Administrative-Contractors/What-is-a-MAC.
35. MPIM, *supra* note 1, Ch. 1, section 1.3.5, and Ch. 3, section 3.2.1.

cal review activities on CERT and Recovery Auditor-identified vulnerabilities.[36]

1. Targeted Probe and Educate

The MACs' current medical review focus is to engage in Targeted Probe and Educate (TPE) audits. When data analysis suggests a *provider- or supplier-specific error* (based on the provider's or supplier's history of high claim error rate or unusual billing patterns), and the items and services billed have high national error rates, a MAC may initiate a TPE audit.[37] In addition to data analysis, providers and suppliers may be selected for TPE audit based on referral from a Recovery Auditor, CERT auditor, UPIC, Office of Inspector General (OIG) or Government Accountability Office (GAO). Beginning first as a demonstration program, on October 1, 2017, TPE was expanded to all MAC jurisdictions. CMS has attempted to assuage providers' concerns regarding an additional audit initiative by assuring that, "Most providers will never need TPE."[38] "Providers/Suppliers and the specific items and services included in the TPE process are those who have been identified through data analysis as being a potential risk to the Medicare trust fund and/or who vary significantly from their peers."[39] The purposes of TPE audits are to decrease provider burden, reduce appeals, and improve the medical review process.[40] The goal of TPE is to quickly rectify claim errors.[41]

---

36. *See id*. Ch. 1, section 1.3.1, and Ch. 3, section 3.2.1.

37. https://www.cms.gov/Research-Statistics-Data-and-Systems/Monitoring-Programs/Medicare-FFS-Compliance-Programs/Medical-Review/Targeted-Probe-and-EducateTPE.

38. *Id.*

39. https://www.cms.gov/Research-Statistics-Data-and-Systems/Monitoring-Programs/Medicare-FFS-Compliance-Programs/Medical-Review/Downloads/TPE-QAs.pdf.

40. MPIM, *supra* note 1, Ch. 3, section 3.2.5.

41. https://www.cms.gov/Research-Statistics-Data-and-Systems/Monitoring-Programs/Medicare-FFS-Compliance-Programs/Medical-Review/Targeted-Probe-and-EducateTPE

Once a MAC has selected a provider or supplier to undergo a TPE audit, it sends the provider/supplier a notification letter outlining the TPE process. The notification letter notes that the provider/supplier will have the opportunity for education and discussion following each round of medical review. The notification letter also lists the repercussions for a provider's or supplier's failure to improve its error rate during the process, including a reminder that, "42 C.F.R. §424.535 authorizes us to revoke Medicare billing privileges under certain conditions. In particular, we note that per 42 CFR §424.535(a)(8)(ii), CMS has the authority to revoke a currently enrolled provider or supplier's Medicare billing privileges if CMS determines that the provider or supplier has a pattern or practice of submitting claims that fail to meet Medicare requirements."[42]

TPE can be performed either on a post-payment or pre-payment basis. A round of TPE generally involves a review of 20 to 40 claims, although CMS may approve a probe sample of a different size. There are usually three rounds of TPE.[43]

Following a review of the probe sample, the MAC will provide an opportunity for one-on-one education. This education may occur via telephone or webinar. The provider or supplier will be granted the opportunity to ask questions to clarify the findings of the medical review. MACs are required to record their educational activities and report on them monthly to CMS. MACs also are required to document and maintain the results of their education. If the provider or supplier does not accept the opportunity for one-on-one education, the MACs also record and maintain this information for data analysis and possible future reporting.[44]

Following the one-on-one education, the MAC will send the provider/supplier a letter detailing the results of the claims

---

42. MPIM, *supra* note 1, Ch. 3, section 3.2.5. *See also* https://www.cms.gov/Research-Statistics-Data-and-Systems/Monitoring-Programs/Medicare-FFS-Compliance-Programs/Medical-Review/Downloads/TPE-QAs.pdf.
43. *Id.*
44. *Id.*

reviewed. The MAC is required to provide a minimum of 45 days after each educational session before selecting the next probe sample, to allow the provider/supplier sufficient time to adopt and implement the recommendations of the MAC.[45]

A provider or supplier will be released from TPE once it reduces its error rate to a specified goal. If, following three rounds of TPE, a provider or supplier fails to achieve the error rate goal, the provider or supplier will be referred to CMS for additional action, which may include "additional rounds of TPE review, 100 percent prepayment review, extrapolation, referral to a Recovery Auditor and/or referral for revocation."[46]

2. Post-payment and Pre-payment Medical Reviews

Although presently, the MACs' medical review strategy is focused on TPE audits, the MACs are authorized to conduct other types of medical reviews. In all scenarios, if a provider or supplier is selected for MAC medical review, the MAC is required to send the provider or supplier a written notice, advising the provider or supplier of the medical review, the reasons for the medical review, and whether the medical review will be conducted on a post-payment or pre-payment basis.[47]

MACs have the discretion to target areas for medical review for many reasons, including the following:

- High volume or "dramatic change" in the utilization of a particular service;
- High cost (note that the authority of the MACs to target an area of review based on cost differs from Recovery Auditors' authority. Recovery Auditors are specifically instructed that they may not target areas for review due to cost alone);
- High-risk, problem-prone areas; and/or

---

45. *Id.*
46. *Id.*
47. *See id.* Ch. 3, section 3.2.2.

- Recovery Auditor, CERT, OIG, or GAO data. If an area is targeted due to data demonstrating vulnerability supplied by one of these entities, a probe audit is not required.[48]

If a *post-payment* medical review is initiated, a provider or supplier must submit requested medical records within the time frame set forth in the Additional Documentation Request (ADR).[49] MACs have the authority to grant extensions to the stated time frame.[50] If no response is received, MACs will deny the claim as not reasonable and necessary.[51] If the requested documentation is received after a denial has been issued, but within "a reasonable number of days" (e.g., 15 days from the date of denial), the MACs are authorized (but not required) to reopen the claim and consider the documentation submitted.[52] Within 60 calendar days of receiving requested documentation, MACs must make a determination and notify the audited provider or supplier of the review results.[53]

MACs will initiate a targeted *pre-payment* medical review only when there is a likelihood of sustained or high level of payment error. MACs are encouraged to initiate targeted service-specific pre-payment review to prevent improper payments with services identified by the CERT program or by Recovery Auditors as problem areas or problem areas identified by their own data analysis.[54]

If a *pre-payment* medical review is initiated, the provider or supplier must submit requested medical records within the time frame set forth in the ADR.[55] MACs are instructed not to grant extensions to the stated time frame.[56] If no response is received

---

48. *See id.*
49. *See id.* Ch. 3, section 3.2.3.2.
50. *See id.* Ch. 3, section 3.2.3.9.
51. *See id.* Ch. 3, section 3.2.3.8.
52. *See id.* Ch. 3, section 3.2.3.9.
53. *See id.* Ch. 3, section 3.3.1.1.
54. *See id.* Ch. 3, section 3.2.1.
55. *See id.* Ch. 3, section 3.2.3.2.
56. *See id.* Ch. 3, section 3.2.3.9.

within the established time frame, MACs will deny the claim.[57] Also in the pre-payment medical review scenario, if requested documentation is received after a denial has been issued, but within "a reasonable number of days" (e.g., 15 days from the date of denial), MACs are authorized (but not required) to reopen the claim and consider the documentation submitted.[58] Within 60 days of receiving requested documentation, the MACs must make a determination on the claim.[59] In a pre-payment review, the MACs are "encouraged to send a notification letter to the provider but may use a remittance advice to meet this requirement."[60] Therefore, it is essential that providers and suppliers closely monitor RAs for notice of claim determinations when subject to pre-payment medical review. Appeal time frames are initiated by the date of a provider's or supplier's receipt of an initial determination. CMS permits MACs to relay notification of a claim determination via RA (as opposed to mandating that MACs always issue a demand letter following an improper payment determination).

In conducting medical reviews, MACs are required to ensure that coverage determinations are made by licensed registered nurses (RNs), therapists, and physicians; MACs are "encouraged," but not required, to use certified coders to evaluate the correct coding for reviewed claims.[61] At the conclusion of the medical review, MACs are required to send notification of their review results even if no improper payment determination is made.[62]

Following receipt of a demand letter (or RA that serves to notify a provider or supplier of an unfavorable claim determination) issued by a MAC, a health care provider or supplier that has

---

57. *See id.* Ch. 3, section 3.2.3.8.
58. *See id.* Ch. 3, section 3.2.3.9.
59. *See id.* Ch. 3, section 3.3.1.1.
60. *See id.* Ch. 3, section 3.6.4.
61. *See id.* Ch. 3, section 3.3.1.1. Licensed practical nurses (LPNs) who currently work for the MAC are "grandfathered in" and may perform medical reviews; however, the MAC may not hire new LPNs to perform medical reviews. *Id.*
62. *See id.* Ch. 3, section 3.6.4.

received an overpayment determination based on a MAC medical review may appeal the improper payment determination via the five-stage Medicare appeals process outlined in Chapter 2.

C. Supplemental Medical Review Contractor (SMRC) Audits

The Supplemental Medical Review Contractor (SMRC) medical review program is the newest addition to the CMS audit programs. The SMRC is tasked to "perform and/or provide support for a variety of tasks aimed at lowering the improper payment rates and increasing efficiencies of the medical review functions of the Medicare and Medicaid Programs,"[63] ultimately in an effort to reduce payment errors by preventing improper payments.[64] Specific goals of the SMRC audit program include the following:

- Using data analysis, identify provider noncompliance with coverage, coding, billing, and payment policies through data analysis;
- Perform medical review;
- Perform statistical extrapolations; and
- Notify health care providers and suppliers of review findings and make recommendations for provider outreach and education or possible UPIC referral.[65]

SMRC audits are focused on Part A, Part B, and DME claims[66] and are focused on vulnerabilities identified by data analysis,

---

63. https://www.noridiansmrc.com.
64. *See, e.g.,* MPIM, *supra* note 1, Ch. 1, section 1.3.8.
65. *Id.*
66. https://www.noridiansmrc.com.

CERT audits, and other sources (including professional organizations and federal oversight agencies).[67]

The SMRC audit process commences with the SMRC sending an ADR. Significantly, the SMRC is specifically tasked to perform a "large volume" of medical reviews.[68] CMS has not placed ADR limits on the SMRC (as it has with Recovery Auditors).

An audited health care provider or supplier has 30 to 45 days from the date of ADR to submit requested medical records.[69] If the SMRC identifies an improper payment, the MAC will adjust the claim. The audited health care provider or supplier may appeal the improper payment determination through the standard five-stage uniform Part A and Part B appeals process outlined in Chapter 2.

D. Recovery Audits

The Recovery Audit program began under Section 306 of the MMA, which directed HHS to conduct a three-year demonstration program using Recovery Auditors (formerly known as Recovery Audit Contractors (RACs)). The demonstration began in 2005. The purpose of the RAC demonstration was to determine the efficacy of using RACs to identify and correct improper payments (both overpayments and underpayments).[70] The RAC demonstration program was initially limited to the three states with the highest Medicare expenditures (i.e., California, Florida, and New

---

67. http://www.cms.gov/Research-Statistics-Data-and-Systems/Monitoring-Programs/Medicare-FFS-Compliance-Programs/Medical-Review/SMRC.

68. *See, e.g.,* MPIM, *supra* note 1, Ch. 1, section 1.3.1.

69 https://www.noridiansmrc.com/contact/frequently-asked-questions-faqs.

70. *See* Section 306 (a) (3) of the MMA. *See also* STATEMENT OF WORK FOR THE RECOVERY AUDIT CONTRACTORS PARTICIPATING IN THE DEMONSTRATION (NON-MEDICARE SECONDARY PAYER), No. 40700NMSPB, Attachment J-2, *available at* http://www.cms.gov/Research-Statistics-Data-and-Systems/Monitoring-Programs/Medicare-FFS-Compliance-Programs/Recovery-Audit-Program/Downloads/Demonstration-SOW.pdf.

York); it later expanded to include three additional states: Massachusetts, South Carolina, and Arizona.[71] RACs were compensated on a contingency fee basis.[72] The RAC demonstration program was highly successful from the point of view of CMS. At the conclusion of the demonstration program, CMS estimated that the RAC demonstration program cost approximately 20 cents for every dollar returned to the Medicare trust funds.[73]

Section 302 of the Tax Relief and Health Care Act of 2006 made the RAC program permanent and required its expansion nationwide by no later than 2010. Pursuant to the Recovery Audit Statement of Work, the mission of the Recovery Audit program is "to reduce Medicare improper payments through the efficient detection and correction of improper payments." As in the RAC demonstration, improper payments are defined to include both overpayments and underpayments and may result from:

- Incorrect payments;
- Non-covered services;
- Incorrectly coded services (including diagnosis-related group [DRG] miscoding); and
- Duplicate services.[74]

Recovery Auditors continue to be compensated on a contingency fee basis, based on the principal amounts collected from or

71. *See* THE MEDICARE RECOVERY AUDIT CONTRACTOR (RAC) PROGRAM: AN EVALUATION OF THE 3-YEAR DEMONSTRATION (June 2008), at p. 1.
72. *Id.* at p. 13.
73. *Id.* at p. 3.
74. *See* STATEMENT OF WORK FOR THE RECOVERY AUDIT PROGRAM, (November 30, 2016) at p. 15.

returned to providers and suppliers.[75] Contingency fees in the permanent Recovery Audit program range from 10.4 to 14.4 percent.[76]

Initially, the permanent Recovery Audit program was limited to reviewing Medicare Fee-for-Service (FFS; i.e., Medicare Part A and Part B) claims. Section 6411 of the Patient Protection and Affordable Care Act expanded the Recovery Audit program to include Medicare Part C, Part D, and Medicaid claims.[77] The FFS Recovery Audit program is the focus of this chapter.

Recovery Auditors are prohibited from selecting claims at random for review. Recovery Auditors are charged with using data analysis to determine claims likely to contain overpayments (i.e., "targeted review").[78] The *Medicare Program Integrity Manual* states that "[i]n general, Recovery Auditors are responsible for reviewing claims where improper payments have been made or there is a high probability that improper payments were made."[79] Notably, in contrast to MACs, Recovery Auditors are prohibited from targeting claims due to high dollar value alone; however, Recovery Auditors may target claims because they have a high dollar value and contain additional information causing the Recovery Auditor suspicion for improper payment.[80] Once a Recovery Auditor has identified a certain item or service as having a high likelihood of improper payment (and it receives CMS approval to conduct medical review), a Recovery Auditor must notify the pro-

75. *Id.* at p. 16.
76. Recovery Auditing in Medicare Fee-for-Service for Fiscal Year 2016, *available at* https://www.cms.gov/Research-Statistics-Data-and-Systems/Monitoring-Programs/Medicare-FFS-Compliance-Programs/Recovery-Audit-Program/Downloads/FY-2016-Medicare-FFS-Report-Congress.pdf.
77 657 U.S.C. § 6411.
78. *See* STATEMENT OF WORK FOR THE RECOVERY AUDIT PROGRAM (November 30, 2016), *supra* note 74, at p. 16.
79. MPIM, *supra* note 1, Ch. 1, section 1.3.5.
80. *See* STATEMENT OF WORK FOR THE RECOVERY AUDIT PROGRAM (November 30, 2016), *supra* note 74, at p. 16.

vider community of its intent to conduct medical review on the item or service via its website.[81]

Recovery Auditors engage in two types of claim reviews to identify improper payments: automated reviews and complex reviews. An *automated review* is a review of claims data without a review of records.[82] A coverage or coding determination may be conducted via automated review only in cases where there is certainty that a claim includes an overpayment, and a written Medicare policy, article, or coding guideline exists. Other determinations (e.g., duplicate claims, pricing mistakes) may be made through automated review even if no written Medicare policy, article, or coding guideline exists.[83] A *complex review* consists of a review of medical or other records and is used in situations where there is a high probability (but not a certainty) that a claim involves an overpayment.[84]

The complex review process begins with the RAC issuing an ADR. According to the Recovery Audit Statement of Work, "Recovery Auditors shall ensure that processes are developed to minimize provider burden to the greatest extent possible when identifying Medicare improper payments. This may include, but is not limited to, ensuring edit parameters are refined to selecting only those claims with the greatest probability that they are improper and that the number of additional documentation requests do not

---

81. MPIM, *supra* note 1, Ch. 3, section 3.2.2.

82. Generally speaking, the Recovery Audit program involves post-payment medical review. However, Recovery Auditors also participated in an 11-state, three-year Prepayment Review Demonstration program, which began on September 1, 2012. *See generally* PREPAYMENT REVIEW DEMONSTRATION, *available at* http://www.cms.gov/Research-Statistics-Data-and-Systems/Monitoring-Programs/Medicare-FFS-Compliance-Programs/Recovery-Audit-Program/RecoveryAuditPrepaymentReview.html.

83. *See* STATEMENT OF WORK FOR THE RECOVERY AUDIT PROGRAM (November 30, 2016), *supra* note 74, at p. 22.

84. *Id.*

impact the provider's ability to provide care."[85] ADR limits are diversified across claim types (e.g., inpatient, outpatient), and ADR limits are adjusted based on a provider's or supplier's denial rate. Providers with lower denial rates will have lower ADR limits.[86] Recovery Auditors are required to compensate acute care hospitals and long-term care hospitals for the cost of supplying requested medical records.[87]

After receiving an ADR request, a health care provider or supplier has 45 days to return requested medical records.[88] In conducting reviews, Recovery Auditors engage the services of registered nurses or therapists to perform medical necessity reviews and certified coders to perform coding reviews.[89] Recovery Audit medical reviewers are required to comply with all National Coverage Determinations (NCDs), coverage provisions in interpretive manuals, national coverage and coding articles, Local Coverage Determinations (LCDs) and local coverage and coding articles in their respective jurisdictions.[90] Recovery Auditors are also permitted to develop internal written review guidelines.[91] Recovery Auditors are required to complete complex reviews within 30 days from receipt of the response to ADR.[92] Following its review of a claim where the Recovery Auditor has identified an improper payment:

---

85. STATEMENT OF WORK FOR THE RECOVERY AUDIT PROGRAM (November 30, 2016), *supra* note 74, at p. 14.

86. *See* Recovery Audit Program Improvements – Completed (as of October 31, 2016), *available at* https://www.cms.gov/Research-Statistics-Data-and-Systems/Monitoring-Programs/Medicare-FFS-Compliance-Programs/Recovery-Audit-Program/Downloads/Recovery-Audit-Program-Improvements-November-24-2017.pdf.

87. STATEMENT OF WORK FOR THE RECOVERY AUDIT PROGRAM (November 30, 2016), *supra* note 74, at p. 12.

88. *Id.* at p. 19.

89. *Id.* at p. 22.

90. *Id.* at p. 26.

91. *Id.*

92. *Id.* at p. 23.

1. The Recovery Auditor sends a Review Results letter to the audited provider or supplier, notifying the provider or supplier whether an improper payment was identified.[93]

2. If an improper payment is alleged, the provider or supplier is entitled to an informal discussion with the Recovery Auditor (outside of the formal Medicare appeals process), which can be used to attempt to persuade the Recovery Auditor to overturn its finding of improper payment. This process is known as Discussion Period review. Receipt of the Review Results letter triggers a provider's or supplier's right to Discussion Period review.[94] A request for Discussion Period review must be submitted within 30 days of receipt of the Review Results letter. The Recovery Auditor is required to wait 30 days after sending the Review Results letter to the provider or supplier before forwarding the claim to the MAC for adjustment to allow for Discussion Period review.[95] The Recovery Audit Statement of Work specifically requires that if a physician (or a physician employed by the provider) requests to speak to the Recovery Auditor's physician during the Discussion Period, that physician's request must be acted upon.[96] This process is generally referred to as a Peer-to-Peer Discussion.

3. Next, the Recovery Auditor sends an electronic file to the MAC with jurisdiction over the provider. The MAC adjusts the claim and issues a demand letter, triggering the provider or supplier's right to engage in the formal Medicare Part A and Part B appeals process outlined in Chapter 2.[97] Of note, under the Recovery Audit Statement of Work, Recovery Auditors are obligated "to provide support throughout the appeals process," and in particular attend at least 50 per-

---

93. *Id.*
94. *Id.* at p. 30.
95. *Id.* at pp. 30-31.
96. *Id.* at p. 31.
97. *Id.*

cent of Administrative Law Judge (ALJ) hearings that may be held.[98] Accordingly, appellant health care providers and suppliers as well as their legal counsel should expect Recovery Auditor presence and participation at ALJ hearings.

E. Unified Program Integrity Contractor (UPIC) Audits

Before the passage of the Health Insurance Portability and Accountability Act of 1996 (HIPAA), Public Law 104–191, Medicare program integrity responsibilities resided with fiscal intermediaries (with responsibility for Medicare Part A claims) and carriers (with responsibility for Medicare Part B claims).[99] Section 202 of HIPAA added a new section 1893 to the Social Security Act and established the Medicare Integrity Program (MIP).[100] The purpose of the MIP is to "promote the integrity of the [M]edicare program," by entering into contracts with certain entities tasked to identify and correct improper payments, including improper payments that occurred as a result of fraud and abuse.[101] Among other activities, MIP contractors are authorized to:

1. Engage in medical and utilization review as well as fraud review;
2. Audit cost reports;
3. Recover improper payments made;
4. Educate health care providers and suppliers regarding benefit integrity issues; and

---

98. *Id.* at p. 2.
99. *See* MEDICARE PROGRAM; MEDICARE INTEGRITY PROGRAM, FISCAL INTERMEDIARY AND CARRIER FUNCTIONS, AND CONFLICT OF INTEREST REQUIREMENTS, FINAL RULE, 72 Fed. Reg. 48870 (August 24, 2007).
100. 42 U.S.C. § 1395ddd (August 21, 1996).
101. 42 U.S.C. § 1395ddd(a) (August 21, 1996). *See also* 42 C.F.R. § 421.304.

5. Develop a list of durable medical equipment (DME) supplies subject to prior authorization.[102]

As part of the MIP, CMS created Program Safeguard Contractors (PSCs), tasked to identify and investigate potential fraud. There were 18 PSCs, with oversight over specific parts of Medicare (e.g., Part A).[103] Subsequently, the PSCs were transitioned to Zone Program Integrity Contractors (ZPICs) to align the contractors' jurisdictions with those of the MACs.[104]

In 2010, CMS established the Center for Program Integrity (CPI), created with the purpose of aligning CMS program integrity efforts in the Medicare and Medicaid programs.[105] Section 4241 of the Small Business Jobs Act of 2010 requires CMS to use "predictive analytics technologies" to identify improper claims submitted for reimbursement and to prevent payment of such claims.[106] To meet this requirement, in July 2011, CMS created a Fraud Prevention System (FPS), an electronic system that "analyzes Medicare claims data using models of fraudulent behavior, which results in automatic alerts on specific claims and providers, which are then prioritized for program integrity analysts to review and investigate

102. 42 U.S.C. § 1395ddd(b) (August 21, 1996).
103. U.S. GAO, Medicare Program Integrity: Contractors Reported Generating Savings but CMS Could Improve Its Oversight, GAO-14-111 (October 2013) [hereinafter Medicare Program Integrity (October 2013)], *available at* http://www.gao.gov/assets/660/658565.pdf.
104. *Id.*; *see also* U.S. Department of Health and Human Services, The Role of Zone Program Integrity Contractors (ZPICs), Formerly the Program Safeguard Contractors (PSCs), Special Edition MLN Matters Number SE1204 Revised (February 29, 2012), *available at* http://www.cms.gov/Outreach-and-Education/Medicare-Learning-Network-MLN/MLNMattersArticles/downloads/SE1204.pdf.
105. http://www.cms.gov/About-CMS/Components/CPI/Center-for-program-integrity.html.
106. Pub. L. No. 111–240, § 4241, 124 Stat. 2504, 2599–2604 (2010).

as appropriate."[107] PSCs/ZPICs were responsible for investigating referrals from the FPS.[108]

On July 19, 2013, CPI published a "Request for Information," seeking information regarding consolidation of the audit and investigation program integrity functions within the Medicare and Medicaid programs. A new contractor, known as a Unified Program Integrity Contractor (UPIC), was proposed to be created to perform these functions.[109] In 2016, CMS began transitioning the remaining PSCs and ZPICs to UPICs.[110]

There are five UPIC jurisdictions.[111] The UPICs are responsible for preventing, detecting, and deterring fraud, waste, and abuse in the Medicare and Medicaid programs by performing the following proactive and reactive functions:

- Identifying program vulnerabilities;
- Identifying incidents of potential fraud, waste, and abuse and responding to same through appropriate action or referral;
- Investigating allegations of fraud from any source;
- Initiating appropriate administrative actions, such as payment suspensions and revocations if appropriate;

---

107. *See* U.S. GAO, MEDICARE FRAUD PREVENTION: CMS HAS IMPLEMENTED A PREDICTIVE ANALYTICS SYSTEM, BUT NEEDS TO DEFINE MEASURES TO DETERMINE ITS EFFECTIVENESS, GAO-13-104 (October 15, 2012), *available at* http://www.gao.gov/products/GAO-13-104.

108. *See* U.S. GAO, MEDICARE PROGRAM INTEGRITY (October 2013), *supra* note 103.

109. *See* CPI INDUSTRY DAY 2013 (July 26, 2013), Solicitation Number: 07022013, *available at* https://www.fbo.gov/?s=opportunity&mode=form&id=408e8137e17c76a2686ef7af0bb7204b&tab=core&_cview=.

110. *See* Department of Health and Human Services, Office of Inspector General, Enhancements Needed in the Tracking and Collection of Medicare Overpayments Identified by ZPICs and PSCs (September 2017), *available at* https://oig.hhs.gov/oei/reports/oei-03-13-00630.pdf.

111. https://www.cms.gov/Research-Statistics-Data-and-Systems/Monitoring-Programs/Medicare-FFS-Compliance-Programs/Review-Contractor-Directory-Interactive-Map.

- Referring cases of possible fraud to the Office of Inspector General (OIG), Office of Investigations; and
- Referring any provider/supplier to the MAC for outreach and education if appropriate.[112]

UPICs select providers and suppliers for review based on internal investigation via data analysis, CMS' fraud investigation database (FID), and information obtained from the internet and news media. UPICs may also receive leads from external sources (e.g., law enforcement, CMS referrals, and beneficiary complaints).[113]

When a UPIC is performing a medical review for program integrity, the purpose is to look for possible instances of fraud, waste, and abuse rather than primarily to make a coverage or coding determination.[114] In conducting such reviews, the UPIC will determine if patterns or trends exist that raise benefit integrity concerns. Examples of such trends include the following:

- Identical or nearly identical documentation.
- Use of higher-level codes more frequently than expected.
- Hours of billed care per day greater than normally would be expected on a workday.
- Evidence suggesting the documentation has been altered.[115]

Pursuant to the *Medicare Program Integrity Manual*, Chapter 3 ("Verifying Potential Errors and Taking Corrective Actions"), before initiating a post-payment or pre-payment medical review, a UPIC is required to notify the selected provider or supplier in writing and indicate whether the medical review will occur on a post-payment or pre-payment basis.[116] However, note that the

---

112. MPIM, *supra* note 1, Ch. 4, section 4.2.2.
113. *Id.*
114. *See id.* Ch. 4, section 4.3.
115. *Id.*
116. *See id.* Ch. 3, section 3.2.2.

investigative authority of UPICs extends beyond medical review;[117] a provider or supplier will not necessarily receive notice that it is under UPIC benefit integrity (i.e., fraud and abuse) investigation when it is initiated.

In both *post-payment* and *pre-payment* UPIC medical reviews, a provider or supplier must respond to the ADR by the date specified in the correspondence. The UPIC may extend this time frame in the post-payment review scenario. If the UPIC does not receive requested documentation, then the UPIC will deny the claim.[118]

In conducting medical reviews, UPICs "shall ensure that the credentials of their reviewers are consistent with the requirements of their respective SOWs [Statement of Works]," and UPICs have the discretion whether or not to use certified coders in making coding determinations.[119] This discretionary language is significant, as in some cases there may not be licensed or certified professionals rendering a coverage and/or coding determination. Oftentimes, UPICs use statistical sampling and extrapolation to estimate the amount of an overpayment in performing audits.[120] UPICs are required to complete their reviews and notify MACs of review determinations within 60 calendar days of receiving documentation in support of the claims at issue.[121] Whenever a complex review is completed and results in an alleged overpayment, UPICs are required to send a review results letter to the provider or supplier.[122] With respect to pre-payment reviews specifically, at the completion of the medical review, UPICs are "encouraged" to send a review results notification letter to the audited provider or supplier; however, UPICs are authorized to use a RA to satisfy the

---

117. *See generally id*. Ch. 4, section 4.2.2.
118. *See id*. Ch. 3, section 3.2.2.
119. *See id*. Ch. 3, section 3.3.1.1.
120. *See id*. Ch. 3, section 3.5.2.
121. *See id*. Ch. 3, section 3.3.1.1.
122. *See id*. Ch. 3, section 3.6.4.

notification requirement.[123] The UPIC next sends data regarding the alleged overpayment to the MAC, which is responsible for issuing a demand letter.[124] Following receipt of a demand letter from the MAC, a health care provider or supplier may appeal an improper payment determination made through the five-stage appeals process described in Chapter 2.

---

123. *Id.*
124. *Id.*

Chapter 2

Overview of the Medicare Part A and Part B Appeals Process

Section 1869 of the Social Security Act (42 U.S.C. § 1395ff) sets forth the five-stage uniform Medicare appeals process for Medicare Part A and Part B appeals. Regulations implementing this portion of the Social Security Act are codified at 42 C.F.R. Part 405 Subpart I, and Centers for Medicare & Medicaid Services (CMS) sub-regulatory guidance related to Medicare Part A and Part B appeals is set forth in the *Medicare Claims Processing Manual* (CMS Internet-Only Manual 100-04), Chapter 29.[1] The five-stage uniform Medicare Part A and Part B appeals process is outlined below.

As an important initial matter, before submitting any appeal, attorneys must ensure that they have been properly appointed to serve as the appellant's legal representative. A valid appointment of representative (AOR) may be effectuated by completing CMS Form 1696[2] or by completing a written statement satisfying certain criteria. Pursuant to 42 C.F.R. § 405.910(c), an AOR statement must satisfy the following criteria:

---

1. Medicare Claims Processing Manual (MCPM) (CMS Pub. 100-04) [hereinafter MCPM], Ch. 29.
2. http://www.cms.gov/Medicare/CMS-Forms/CMS-Forms/downloads/cms1696.pdf.

1. Be in writing and signed and dated by both the party and individual agreeing to be the representative;
2. Provide a statement appointing the representative to act on behalf of the party, and in the case of a beneficiary, authorizing the adjudicator to release identifiable health information to the appointed representative;
3. Include a written explanation of the purpose and scope of the representation;
4. Contain both the party's and appointed representative's name, phone number, and address;
5. Identify the beneficiary's Medicare health insurance claim number or provider's or supplier's National Provider Identifier (NPI). If the party being represented is the beneficiary, the Medicare number must be included on the AOR. If the party being represented is a provider or supplier, the NPI should be provided.;
6. Include the appointed representative's professional status or relationship to the party; and
7. Be filed with the entity processing the party's initial determination or appeal.[3]

If an AOR submitted with an appeal is defective, the adjudicator is required to contact the representative and provide an opportunity to cure the defect. If the AOR is not corrected, then the representative will be deemed to lack authority to act on behalf of the appellant.[4]

---

3. *See* MCPM, *supra* note 1, Ch. 29, section 270.
4. 42 C.F.R. § 405.910 (d).

A. Stage 1: Redetermination

Following receipt of an initial determination,[5] a party may file a request for "redetermination." A request for redetermination must be submitted in writing to the Medicare Administrative Contractor (MAC) that issued the initial determination. A request for redetermination must be submitted within 120 days following the date of receipt of notice of initial determination (a party will be presumed to have received the notice of initial determination five days after the date of the notice, unless there is evidence to the contrary).[6] An individual who was not involved in making the initial determination must perform the redetermination. In conducting a redetermination, a MAC is authorized to evaluate all evidence submitted and all evidence the MAC obtains on its own.[7] Although federal regulations permit MACs to raise and develop new issues relevant to a claim that is the subject of appeal, through sub-regulatory guidance, CMS has instructed the MACs to limit their review to the reason(s) the claim or line item at issue was initially denied.[8] The MAC is required to conclude its redetermination review no later than the 60-day period beginning on the date the MAC receives the request for redetermination.[9]

---

5. *See* Section 1869(a)(2) of the Social Security Act (42 U.S.C. § 1395ff(a)(2) (December 21, 2000)). *See also* 42 C.F.R. § 405.920 and MCPM, *supra* note 1, Ch. 29, section 200.

6. Section 1869(a)(3)(C)(i) of the Social Security Act (42 U.S.C. § 1395ff(a)(3)(C)(i) (December 21, 2000)). *See also* 42 C.F.R. § 405.942 (a) and MCPM, *supra* note 1, Ch. 29, section 310.2.

7. 42 C.F.R. § 405.948. *See also* MCPM, *supra* note 1, Ch. 29, section 310.4.

8. *Id. See also* MLN Matters Number SE1521, "Limiting the Scope of Review on Redeterminations and Reconsiderations of Certain Claims," Revision date May 9, 2016, *available at* https://www.cms.gov/Outreach-and-Education/Medicare-Learning-Network-MLN/MLNMattersArticles/Downloads/SE1521.pdf.

9. Section 1869(a)(3)(C)(ii) of the Social Security Act (42 U.S.C. § 1395ff(a)(3)(C)(ii) (December 21, 2000)). *See also* 42 C.F.R. § 405.950 and MCPM, *supra* note 1, Ch. 29, section 310.4.

1. Recoupment during Redetermination

Section 935(f)(2)(A) of the MMA amended section 1893 of the Social Security Act (42 U.S.C. § 1395ddd) to prohibit Medicare contractors from recouping an alleged overpayment until after a reconsideration decision has been issued. Through its implementing regulations, CMS requires an appellant to meet expedited appeals time frames to avoid withhold or recoupment of an alleged overpayment during the first two stages of appeal. Interest accrues against the alleged overpayment.[10]

Although health care providers and suppliers have 120 days from the date of receipt of a demand letter to submit a request for redetermination, a MAC may initiate withholding of Medicare reimbursements as payment against the alleged overpayment if a request for redetermination is not submitted within 40 days of the date of the demand letter. If this time frame is not satisfied and the MAC begins withholding, it will cease recoupment efforts once it receives a redetermination request.[11]

---

10. *See* MEDICARE FINANCIAL MANAGEMENT MANUAL (MFMM) (CMS Pub. 100-06), Ch. 3, section 200.6, *available at* http://www.cms.gov/Regulations-and-Guidance/Guidance/Manuals/Downloads/fin106c03.pdf.

Notably, in order to avoid assessment of interest to an alleged overpayment, many providers and suppliers have requested immediate offset of the alleged overpayment, resulting in immediate recoupment of the alleged overpayment. In these cases, the recoupment is considered "voluntary" and the appellant does not receive Section 935 interest if the overpayment is reversed as part of the appeals process. *See* MLN Matters Number MM 7688 Revised, "Immediate Recoupment for Fee for Service Claims Overpayments," Revised February 10, 2012, *available at* https://cms.gov/Outreach-and-Education/Medicare-Learning-Network-MLN/MLNMattersArticles/downloads/MM7688.pdf.

11. *See* 42 C.F.R. § 405.379(d) and MLN Matters Number MM 6183 Revised, "Limitation on Recoupment 935 for Provider, Physicians and Suppliers Overpayments," Revised February 15, 2018, *available at* https://www.cms.gov/Outreach-and-Education/Medicare-Learning-Network-MLN/MLNMattersArticles/downloads/MM6183.pdf.

B. Stage 2: Reconsideration

If a party is dissatisfied with a redetermination decision, it may file a request for "reconsideration."[12] A request for reconsideration must be submitted in writing to the qualified independent contractor (QIC) identified in the redetermination decision.[13] A request for reconsideration must be submitted within 180 days from the date the party receives notice of a partially favorable or unfavorable redetermination decision (a party will be presumed to have received the redetermination decision five days after the date of the notice, unless there is evidence to the contrary).[14] Of significance to appellants, federal regulations require all evidence to be submitted at the reconsideration stage of review. If an appellant fails to do so, absent good cause, new evidence may not be submitted at subsequent stages of appeal.[15] Unless good cause is shown, the Administrative Law Judges (ALJs), Medicare Appeals Council ("Council"), and federal district court will limit their review to the evidence submitted at or before reconsideration.

When an appealed claim involves a medical necessity determination, the QIC designates a panel of physicians or other appropriate health care professionals to participate in the medical review. Where a claim pertains to treatment, items, or services rendered by a physician, the reviewing professional must be a physician.[16] As with redeterminations, in conducting a reconsideration review, federal regulations authorize the QICs to raise and develop new issues it deems to be relevant to the claims at issue; however, via

---

12. *See* Section 1869(b)(1) of the Social Security Act (42 U.S.C. § 1395ff(b)(1) (December 21, 2000)). *See also* 42 C.F.R § 405.960 and MCPM, *supra* note 1, Ch. 29, section 320.
13. *See* 42 C.F.R. § 405.964 and MCPM, *supra* note 1, Ch. 29, section 320.1.
14. *See* Section 1869(b)(1)(D)(i) of the Social Security Act (42 U.S.C. § 1395ff(b)(1)(D)(i) (December 21, 2000)). *See also* 42 C.F.R. § 405.962 and MCPM, *supra* note 1, Ch. 29, section 320.2.
15. 42 C.F.R. § 405.966.
16. 42 C.F.R. § 405.968(c).

sub-regulatory guidance, CMS has instructed the QICs to limit their reconsideration reviews to the reason(s) the claim or line item at issue was initially denied.[17] While the QIC is bound by any applicable National Coverage Determination (NCD),[18] it is not bound by Local Coverage Determinations (LCDs), Local Medical Review Policies (LMRPs) or CMS program guidance, but will give substantial guidance to such policies in rendering a decision.[19] The QIC is required to conclude its reconsideration review no later than 60 days following the date it receives the reconsideration request.[20] If the QIC fails to abide by this time frame, a party may "escalate" its appeal to the ALJ stage of appeal, in essence bypassing the QIC reconsideration review.[21]

1. Recoupment during Reconsideration

To avoid recoupment and/or withholding of Medicare payments during the reconsideration stage of appeal, a provider or supplier that receives a partially favorable or unfavorable redetermination decision must submit its request for reconsideration within 60 days of the date of redetermination decision (rather than 180 days from receipt of the redetermination decision). Recoupment may commence on day 61 if no appeal is submitted. Recoupment will stop

17. 42 C.F.R. § 968(b) and *see also* MLN Matters Number SE1521, "Limiting the Scope of Review on Redeterminations and Reconsiderations of Certain Claims," Revised May 9, 2016, *available at* https://www.cms.gov/Outreach-and-Education/Medicare-Learning-Network-MLN/MLNMattersArticles/Downloads/SE1521.pdf.
18. 42 C.F.R. § 968(b).
19. *Id.*
20. *See* Section 1869(c)(3)(C)(i) of the Social Security Act (42 U.S.C. § 1395ff(c)(3)(C)(i) (December 8, 2003)). *See also* 42 C.F.R. § 405.970 and MCPM, *supra* note 1, Ch. 29, section 320.
21. *See* Section 1869(c)(3)(C)(ii) of the Social Security Act (42 U.S.C. § 1395ff(c)(3)(C)(ii) (December 21, 2000)). *See also* 42 C.F.R. § 405.970(d) and MCPM, *supra* note 1, Ch. 29, section 330.

once a request for reconsideration is received.[22] This expedited time frame could create challenges for those attempting to obtain additional documentation in support of an appeal to submit with a request for reconsideration (to abide by the requirement for early presentation of evidence).[23]

Following receipt of a partially favorable or unfavorable reconsideration decision, CMS is permitted to begin withholding Medicare payments against the alleged overpayment.[24]

C. Stage 3: ALJ Hearing

If a party is dissatisfied with a reconsideration decision, it may file a request for ALJ hearing with the Department of Health and Human Services (HHS) Office of Medicare Hearings and Appeals (OMHA).[25] An appellant's request for ALJ hearing must be submitted within 60 days of the date of a party's receipt of reconsideration decision (a party will be presumed to have received the reconsideration decision five days after the date of the notice, unless there is evidence to the contrary).[26] An amount in contro-

---

22. *See* 42 C.F.R. § 405.379(e) and MLN Matters Number MM6183 Revised, "Limitation on Recoupment 935 for Provider, Physicians and Suppliers Overpayments," Revised February 15, 2018, *available at* https://www.cms.gov/Outreach-and-Education/Medicare-Learning-Network-MLN/MLNMatters Articles/downloads/MM6183.pdf.

23. *See* 42 C.F.R. § 405.966 and MLN Matters Number MM 6183 Revised, "Limitation on Recoupment 935 for Provider, Physicians and Suppliers Overpayments," Revised February 15, 2018, *available at* https://www.cms.gov/Outreach-and-Education/Medicare-Learning-Network-MLN/MLNMatters Articles/downloads/MM6183.pdf.

24. *Id.*

25. Section 1869(b)(1) of the Social Security Act (42 U.S.C. § 1395ff(b)(1) (December 21, 2000)). *See also* 42 C.F.R. § 405.1000 and MCPM, *supra* note 1, Ch. 29, section 330.

26. 42 C.F.R. § 405.1002 and MCPM, *supra* note 1, Ch. 29, section 330.

versy requirement applies.[27] For appearances by individuals other than unrepresented beneficiaries, an ALJ hearing will be conducted by telephone (unless the judge finds good cause to conduct the hearing via video teleconference or in person).[28]

In conducting its hearing, the ALJ is bound by provisions of any applicable NCD.[29] On the other hand, the ALJ is not bound by LCDs, LMRPs or CMS program guidance, but will give substantial guidance to such policies in rendering a decision.[30] The Social Security Act expressly requires that an ALJ "conduct and conclude a hearing on a decision of a qualified independent contractor . . . and render a decision on such hearing by not later than the end of the 90-day period beginning on the date a request for hearing has been timely filed."[31] If the ALJ fails to abide by this time frame, a party may "escalate" its appeal to the Council for review.[32]

There are circumstances where the statutory 90-day adjudication period for ALJ appeals is extended. In some cases, these exceptions could result in a significant adjudication delay. For example:

- If an appeal is escalated to the ALJ stage of appeal from the QIC reconsideration stage of appeal, the ALJ is required to

---

27. *See* Section 1869(b)(1)(E) of the Social Security Act (42 U.S.C. § 1395ff(b)(1)(E) (December 21, 2000)). *See also* 42 C.F.R. § 405.1006 and MCPM, *supra* note 1, Ch. 29, section 330. For calendar year 2021, the amount in controversy must be at least $180. *See* 85 Fed. Reg. 60795 (September 28, 2020) and http://www.cms.gov/Medicare/Appeals-and-Grievances/MMCAG/ALJ.html.

28. 42 C.F.R. § 1020(b). For appearances by unrepresented beneficiaries, the ALJ hearing will be conducted via video teleconference, unless the judge finds that a telephone hearing may be more convenient for the unrepresented beneficiary, or in person if video teleconference or phone technology is unavailable or other special or extraordinary circumstances exist. 42 C.F.R. § 1020 (a).

29. 42 C.F.R. § 1060.

30. 42 C.F.R. § 405.1062.

31. *See* Section 1869(d)(1)(A) of the Social Security Act (42 U.S.C. § 1395ff(d)(1)(A) (December 21, 2000)). *See also* 42 C.F.R. § 405.1016 and MCPM, *supra* note 1, Ch. 29, section 330.1.

32. *See* Section 1869(d)(3)(A) of the Social Security Act (42 U.S.C. § 1395ff(d)(3)(A) (December 21, 2000)). *See also* 42 C.F.R. § 405.1106 and MCPM, *supra* note 1, Ch. 29, section 340.

issue its decision "no later than the end of the 180-calendar day period beginning on the date that the request for escalation is received by the ALJ hearing office."[33]

- If an appellant submits additional evidence not included with the request for ALJ hearing later than 10 calendar days after receiving the notice of hearing, "the period between the time the evidence was required to have been submitted and the time it is received is not counted toward the adjudication deadline."[34]

- If an appellant fails to send a notice of its ALJ hearing request to the other parties who received a copy of the QIC's decision, the 90-day adjudication period is tolled until all parties are notified of an appellant's request for ALJ hearing.[35]

1. ALJ Backlog and Resolution

Over the past decade, aggressive Medicare audit activity led to a significant increase in the volume of claim denials made, and by extension requests for ALJ hearings submitted, resulting in an inability for OMHA to timely adjudicate pending appeals. Although in Fiscal Year (FY) 2009, the average processing time for a request for ALJ hearing was 94.9 days (near the statutory time frame for processing), by FY 2020 the average processing time for a request for ALJ hearing had ballooned to 1,447.6 days.[36] OMHA simply did not have the manpower to process the volume of appeals filed. In response to a lawsuit filed by the American Hospital Association (AHA), together with three plaintiff hospitals

---

33. 42 C.F.R. § 405.1016(c).

34. 42 C.F.R. § 405.1018.

35. 42 C.F.R. § 405.1014(b)(2).

36. https://www.hhs.gov/about/agencies/omha/about/current-workload/average-processing-time-by-fiscal-year/index.html. By way of further illustration, in FY 2015, there were 886,418 appeals pending at the OMHA stage of review. This number decreased to 201,292 appeals pending at the OMHA stage of review in FY 2020. *See* Medicare Appeals Dashboard, *available at* https://www.aha.org/system/files/media/file/2020/09/alj-delay-status-dashboard-medicare-appeals-9-24-20.pdf.

affected by the backlog, on November 1, 2018, the United States District Court for the District of Columbia ordered HHS to resolve the backlog of pending appeals by the end of FY 2022.[37]

Over the years, OMHA pursued a multi-pronged approach to address the backlog:

1. Invest new resources at all levels of appeal to increase adjudication capacity and implement new strategies to alleviate the current backlog.
2. Take administrative actions to reduce the number of pending appeals and encourage resolution earlier in the process.
3. Propose legislative reforms that provide additional funding and new authorities to address the appeals volume.[38]

Regarding items 1 and 3 above, in 2018, OMHA received additional funding, such that it was able to expand its workforce to effectively chip away at the backlog of pending appeals.[39] Regarding item 2, OMHA has offered certain opportunities for appellants to resolve a large number of pending appeals: (1) a statistical sampling initiative and (2) a settlement conference facilitation program.

2. Statistical Sampling Initiative

The statistical sampling initiative is a program designed to provide appellants with an option to address large volumes of claim disputes pending at the ALJ level of appeal. In the statistical sampling initiative, a "trained and experienced statistical expert" will first

---

37. American Hospital Association v. Azar, 2018 WL 572314 (D.D.C. November 1, 2018). For an in-depth discussion concerning the Medicare appeals backlog and resolution, *see* Jessica L. Gustafson, Esq. and Abby Pendleton, Esq., *District Court Rules OMHA Appeals Backlog to Be Eliminated by 2022,* A.B.A. THE HEALTH LAWYER, Vol. 31, No. 3, February 2019.
38. FACT SHEET: HHS Issues Final Rule to Improve the Medicare Appeals Process, *available at* https://www.hhs.gov/sites/default/files/medicare-appeals-final-rule-fact-sheet-jan2017.pdf.
39. *American Hospital Association,* 2018 WL 572314 at *3.

develop appropriate sampling methodology in compliance with Medicare guidance. The statistical expert will randomly select the sampling units for the ALJ to ultimately review.[40]

Use of the statistical sampling initiative may be initiated by an appellant or offered by OMHA. The appellant must be a single Medicare provider or supplier (or owned by a single entity). Eligible claims include those that do not have a hearing date scheduled. The universe of claims to be sampled must total at least 250, falling into only one of the following categories: (1) pre-payment claim denials; (2) post-payment (overpayment) non-RAC claim denials; or (3) post-payment (overpayment) RAC claim denials from one Recovery Auditor.[41]

An ALJ will hold a pre-hearing conference to obtain consent for sampling and to address any other matters to facilitate the hearing. Next, the ALJ will issue a pre-hearing order. After the pre-hearing order is issued and becomes binding, at this point, an appellant may no longer withdraw its consent to engage in the statistical sampling initiative. All appeals will be combined into a single appeal and assigned to a new ALJ. The ALJ will review the sample units and make findings on those units. A CMS contractor will then extrapolate the ALJ's decision to the universe of claims.[42]

3. Settlement Conference Facilitation Pilot

The Settlement Conference Facilitation (SCF) pilot is an alternative dispute resolution process "designed to bring the appellant and [CMS] together to discuss the potential of a mutually agreeable resolution for claims appealed to the [ALJ] hearing level."[43] SCF is limited to pending requests for OMHA ALJ hearing that were filed

---

40. https://www.hhs.gov/about/agencies/omha/about/special-initiatives/statistical-sampling/index.html.

41. https://www.hhs.gov/sites/default/files/ST-4256_OHMA%20website%20Stat%20sample%20Fact%20Sheet%206-2_remediated%20.pdf.

42. Id.

43. https://www.hhs.gov/about/agencies/omha/about/special-initiatives/settlement-conference-facilitation/index.html.

on or before March 31, 2020. The beneficiary may not have participated in the reconsideration. SCF is completely voluntary; any party may decline to participate at any time. If, after submitting an expression of interest, CMS agrees to SCF, the SCF will involve all of the appellant's pending appeals associated with its NPI.[44]

Appellants with appealed claims that have billed amounts (or extrapolated overpayment amounts) of $100,000 or less are eligible for a process known as SCF Express. In this process, if CMS agrees to participate in SCF, it will provide a settlement offer to the appellant based on preliminary data at its disposal (such as the appellant's appeals success rate and the type of item(s) or service(s) at issue), without undergoing a formal mediation process. Appellants with less than $10,000 total in billed charges are only able to participate in SCF Express. If the appellant accepts CMS's settlement offer, it must respond within seven calendar days by signing and returning the proposed settlement agreement. If the appellant does not wish to accept CMS's SCF Express settlement offer, it may so notify CMS and proceed to SCF.[45]

Appellants with appealed claims that have billed amounts (or extrapolated overpayment amounts) of $100,000 or more, and appellants with appealed claims that have billed amounts of $10,000 or more that have declined a SCF Express settlement offer, are eligible to proceed to settlement conference. OMHA will first conduct a pre-settlement conference, at which the parties will agree to a deadline for any position paper submission and discuss possible dates for the settlement conference. At the conference, for those appellants with appealed claims that have billed amounts (or an extrapolated overpayment) of $100,000 or less, if an agreement is reached, both parties will sign the settlement agreement at the conclusion of the settlement conference. If the appellant has appealed claims with billed amounts (or an extrapolated overpayment) of $100,000 or more, if the parties agree to a settlement per-

---

44. *Id.*
45. *Id.*

centage, they will forward the proposed settlement agreement to CMS for approval prior to signing. If an agreement is not reached, the appeals will be returned to the previously assigned adjudicator or be placed back in queue awaiting hearing.[46]

D. Stage 4: Medicare Appeals Council (the "Council") Review

If a party is dissatisfied with an ALJ's decision, it may file a request for Council review.[47] A request for Council review must be submitted in writing within 60 days of the date of a party's receipt of the ALJ decision (a party will be presumed to have received the ALJ decision five days after the date of the notice, unless there is evidence to the contrary).[48] The Council's review of an appellant's review of a decision or dismissal is de novo,[49] meaning the Council will engage in a fresh look at the appeal. In addition, the Council may decide on its own motion to review an ALJ's decision or dismissal. CMS may request that the MAC take review on its own motion if CMS or its contractor participated in the ALJ hearing, and "in CMS' view, the ALJ's decision or dismissal is not supported by the preponderance of evidence in the record or the ALJ abused his or her discretion." Moreover, CMS or any of its contractors (including the Administrative QIC (AdQIC), the entity tasked to serve as the clearinghouse for all Part A and Part B claims[50]) may refer a case to the Council anytime within 60 calendar days from the date of the ALJ's decision or dismissal "if, in their view, the decision or dismissal contains an error of law material to the out-

---

46. *Id.*
47. Section 1869(b)(1) of the Social Security Act (42 U.S.C. § 1395ff(b)(1) (December 21, 2000)). *See also* 42 C.F.R. § 405.1100 and MCPM, *supra* note 1, Ch. 29, section 340.
48. *See* 42 C.F.R. § 405.1102 and MCPM, *supra* note 1, Ch. 29, section 340.
49. 42 C.F.R. § 405.1100.
50. MCPM, *supra* note 1, Ch. 29, section 330.3.

come of the claim or presents a broad policy or procedural issue that may affect the public interest."[51]

A party may request to appear before the Council to present oral argument. The Council may accept such a request to present oral argument if the case raises an important question of law, policy, or fact that cannot be readily decided based on written submissions alone.[52] The Council is required to conduct and conclude a review of the decision on an ALJ hearing and make a decision (or remand the case to the ALJ) in 90 days.[53] If the Council fails to issue its decision within this time frame, a party may "escalate" its appeal to federal district court.[54]

E. Stage 5: Federal District Court Review

If a party is dissatisfied with the Council decision, it may file a request for federal district court review.[55] An amount in controversy requirement applies.[56] In a federal district court action, the findings of fact by HHS are deemed conclusive if supported by substantial evidence.[57]

---

51. 42 C.F.R. § 405.1110.

52. 42 C.F.R. § 405.1124.

53. *See* Section 1869(d)(2)(A) of the Social Security Act (42 U.S.C. § 1395ff(d)(2)(A) (December 21, 2000)) and 42 C.F.R. § 405.1100.

54. *See* Section 1869(d)(3)(B) of the Social Security Act (42 U.S.C. § 1395ff(d)(3)(B)) (December 21, 2000) and 42 C.F.R. § 405.1132.

55. *See* Section 1869(b)(1) of the Social Security Act (42 U.S.C. § 1395ff(b)(1) (December 21, 2000)). *See also* 42 C.F.R. § 405.1136 and MCPM, *supra* note 1, Ch. 29, section 345.

56. *See* Section 1869(b)(1)(E) of the Social Security Act (42 U.S.C. § 1395ff(b)(1)(E) (December 21, 2000)). *See also* 42 C.F.R. §§ 405.1006(c) and 405.1136(a), as well as MCPM, *supra* note 1, Ch. 29, section 340. For calendar year 2014, the amount in controversy threshold is $1,430. *See* 78 Fed. Reg. 59702 (September 27, 2013) and http://www.cms.gov/Medicare/Appeals-and-Grievances/OrgMedFFSAppeals/Review-Federal-District-Court.html.

57. *See* 42 C.F.R. § 405.1136(f).

In addition, in certain circumstances, Medicare providers and suppliers may obtain expedited access to judicial review (EAJR).[58] EAJR may be granted in lieu of an ALJ hearing or Council review if a review entity (comprised of up to three reviewers who are ALJs or members of the Department Appeals Board) certifies that the Council does not have authority to decide a question of law or regulation and no material facts are in dispute.[59] If there is more than one party to the reconsideration, ALJ hearing, or Council review, each must concur in writing with the request for EAJR.[60] The review entity has 60 days to issue a certification for EAJR or to deny the request.[61] If the review entity fails to act within this time frame, the appellant may bring a civil action in federal district court within 60 days of the expiration of this time period.[62] A review entity's decision to certify EAJR or deny the request is not subject to review by HHS.[63]

---

58. *See* Section 1869(b)(2) of the Social Security Act (42 U.S.C. § 1395ff(b)(2) (December 21, 2000)). *See also* 42 C.F.R. § 405.990.

59. *See* Section 1869(b)(2) of the Social Security Act (42 U.S.C. § 1395ff(b)(2) (December 21, 2000)). *See also* 42 C.F.R. § 405.990(a)(2).

60. *See* 42 C.F.R. § 405.990(a)(4).

61. *See* 42 C.F.R. § 405.990(f)(2).

62. *See* 42 C.F.R. § 405.990(f)(4).

63. *See* 42 C.F.R. § 405.990(f)(3).

Chapter 3

Legal Challenges to Part A and Part B Audit Determinations

If a health care provider or supplier receives an improper payment determination resulting from a Medicare audit, many strategies exist that can be successfully employed in the Medicare Part A and Part B appeals process to effectuate meaningful results. Historically, health care providers' and suppliers' success in the appeals process has varied by level of appeal. A November 2012 Report by the Office of Inspector General (OIG) reported that the QICs issued fully favorable results in 20 percent of cases decided at reconsideration. Fully favorable ALJ decisions were issued in 56 percent of cases decided, and partially favorable ALJ decisions were issued in an additional 6 percent of cases.[1] The OIG reported variances in appeals results based on claim type and appellant, with Part A inpatient hospital appeals having the highest appeals success rate at

---

1. OIG Report, "Improvements Are Needed at the Administrative Law Judge Level of Medicare Appeals" (OEI-02-10-00340) [hereinafter "Improvements Are Needed"] at p. 12, November 14, 2012, *available at* https://oig.hhs.gov/oei/reports/oei-02-10-00340.asp. *See also* https://www.hhs.gov/about/agencies/omha/about/current-workload/decision-statistics/index.html, setting forth "decision statistics." Note that OMHA's more current reported decision statistics suggest a downward trend in fully favorable ALJ decisions.

72 percent.[2] Appeals strategies that have proven successful include advocating the merits of the underlying claims and employing legal challenges.

Throughout this chapter, Council decisions have been cited and summarized to illustrate the way in which the Council has addressed appellants' arguments. However, note that Council decisions are binding only on the parties to a particular appeal, and they do not have precedential value unless the Chair of the Department Appeals Board (DAB) designates a Council decision as precedential. The cited Council decisions have not been designated as precedential.[3]

A. Advocating the Merits

When advocating the merits of a claim, it is valuable to draft a position paper outlining factual and legal arguments in support of payment. Medical summaries, illustrations (e.g., color-coded charts, graphs and other visual representations) are user-friendly for the decision maker and may prove valuable in the appeals process. It is also beneficial to engage the services of a qualified expert, both in cases involving medical necessity and cases involving coding, to prepare written statements and present oral argument.

---

2. *Id.*

3. 82 Fed. Reg. 4974 at 4978 (January 17, 2017), *available at* https://www.gov info.gov/content/pkg/FR-2017-01-17/pdf/2016-32058.pdf. *See also* 42 C.F.R. § 401.109. Notice of decisions designated as precedential will be made through the Federal Register and posted on a page of HHS's website. 82 Fed. Reg. at 4978. As of March 2021, no Council decisions have been designated as precedential.

B. Treating Physician Rule

Pursuant to Section 1862 (a) of the Social Security Act,[4] payment may not be made under Medicare Part A or Part B for items or services that "are not reasonable and necessary for the diagnosis or treatment of illness or injury or to improve the functioning of a malformed body member." In many audit situations, a medical review contractor will render an unfavorable initial determination, alleging that the items or services rendered were not medically necessary. Such determinations are oftentimes subjective and subject to rigorous challenge by an affected health care provider or supplier.

Pursuant to Section 1801 of the Social Security Act:[5]

> Nothing in this subchapter shall be construed to authorize any Federal officer or employee to exercise any supervision or control over the practice of medicine or the manner in which medical services are provided, or over the selection, tenure, or compensation of any officer or employee of any institution, agency or person providing health services; or to exercise any supervision or control over the administration or operation of any such institution, agency or person.

Based on this portion of the law, an argument can be made that a treating physician's judgment that a service is medically necessary is entitled to deference over that of a nonphysician medical review contractor. The "treating physician rule" is a legal doctrine, first applied to Social Security Disability benefits cases, reflecting the principle that a treating physician's determination that a service is medically necessary is binding unless contradicted by substantial evidence and is entitled to some extra weight, even if contradicted, because the treating physician is inherently more familiar with the patient's medical condition than a retrospective reviewer. In sum-

---

4. 42 U.S.C. § 1395y (a) (July 30, 1965).
5. 42 U.S.C. § 1395 (July 30, 1965).

mary, the "treating physician rule" is the legal theory that a treating physician's determination that a service is medically necessary and appropriate should predominate over a reviewer's determination.

1. HCFA Ruling 93-1

The "treating physician rule's" applicability to cases involving Medicare coverage has been varied. In 1993, the Health Care Financing Administration (HCFA), now CMS, issued HCFA Ruling 93-1. The purpose statement for the Ruling is as follows:

> This Ruling clarifies the position of the Health Care Financing Administration (HCFA) concerning the weight to be given to a treating physician's opinion in determining coverage of inpatient hospital and skilled nursing facility care. (This Ruling does not by omission or implication endorse the application of the treating physician rule to those types of services that are not discussed in this Ruling).

In summary, the Ruling states that "It is HCFA's Ruling that no presumptive weight should be assigned to the treating physician's medical opinion in determining the medical necessity of inpatient hospital or SNF services under section 1862(a)(1) of the Act. A physician's opinion will be evaluated in the context of the evidence in the complete administrative record."

Significantly, the Ruling specifically applies to Part A claims, and does not prohibit the "treating physician rule" from applying to other types of claims (e.g., Part B claims).[6] Furthermore,

---

6. *See, e.g.,* Precision Therapeutics v. Sebelius, 2010 WL 3924323 (W.D. Pa. 2010); Executive Director of Office of Vermont Health Access ex rel. Carey v. Sebelius, 698 F. Supp. 2d 436 (D. Vt. 2010); U.S. v. Prabhu, 442 F. Supp. 2d 1008 (D. Nev. 2006): Dennis v. Shalala, 1994 WL 708166 (D. Vt. 1994) (all applying the "treating physician rule" following publication of HCFA Ruling 93-1). *See also* Almy v. Sebelius, 749 F. Supp. 2d 315 (D. Md. 2010), FN 10 and Diapulse Corp. of America v. Sebelius, 2010 WL 1037250 (E.D.N.Y. 2010) (declining to extend application of the "treating physician rule" to cases concerning Medicare

although the Ruling does not extend presumptive weight to a treating physician's medical opinion in determining the medical necessity of inpatient hospital or SNF services, the Ruling acknowledges that in "the vast majority of cases, the attending physician's certification of the medical need for the services is consistent with other records submitted in support of the claim for payment, the claim is paid . . . [C]riteria recognize the medical judgments may not always be clear cut at any given point in time and permit reasonable leeway in questionable situations, as long as the evaluation is diligent and ongoing. . . . We note that the criteria governing how the medical review entity makes its determination do not discount the role of the treating physician." Especially in situations where appellant providers or suppliers are challenging a Medicare Part B determination, the "treating physician rule" should be raised in defense of the medical necessity of the claim at issue.

C. Waiver of Liability

Under the legal theory of "waiver of liability," when a Medicare contractor determines that an item or service was not medically necessary under Section 1862 of the Social Security Act (resulting

---

coverage). In addition, the Medicare Appeals Council (Council) has applied the "treating physician rule" in the following cases:
- *In the case of Sacred Heart Hospital* (November 10, 2009)—In deciding this Part A case, the Council found that it was bound by HCFA Ruling 93-1 and the "treating physician rule" did not apply.
- *In the case of Maximum Comfort, Inc.* (September 29, 2003)—In this case, the Council referenced HCFA Ruling 93-1, acknowledged that the Ruling specifically applied to Part A cases, but noted that even if the Council were to apply the "treating physician rule" to the facts of the at issue Part B case, it would provide no relief to the Appellant.

in a denial of payment),[7,8] in situations where the provider or supplier did not know, or could not have been reasonably expected to know, that payment would not be made, then the provider or supplier is nonetheless entitled to reimbursement for the item or service provided.

The statutory authority for application of "waiver of liability" is set forth in Section 1879 of the Social Security Act,[9] which states in relevant part:

> Where—
> (1) a determination is made that, by reason of Section 1862 (a) (1) or (9) or by reason of a coverage denial described in subsection (g), payment may not be made under Part A or Part B of this title for any expenses incurred for items or services furnished an individual by a provider of services or by another person pursuant to an assignment under section 1842 (b) (3) (B) (ii); and
> (2) both such individual and such provider of services or such other person, as the case may be, did not know, and could not reasonably have expected to know, that payment would not be made for such items or services under Part A or B,

---

7. Pursuant to Section 1862(a) of the Social Security Act (42 U.S.C. § 1395y) (July 30, 1965), payment may not be made under Medicare Part A or Part B for items or services that "are not reasonable and necessary for the diagnosis or treatment of illness or injury or to improve the functioning of a malformed body member."

8. Notably, the legal theory of "waiver of liability" is inapplicable to technical denials (e.g., a denial of payment for SNF stay because the beneficiary did not have a three-day hospital stay first; a denial of payment for home health services because they were not ordered on a plan of treatment; etc.). *See* MEDICARE CLAIMS PROCESSING MANUAL (MCPM) (CMS Pub. 100-04) [hereinafter MCPM], Ch. 29, section 20.2.2.

9. 42 U.S.C. § 1395pp (August 5, 1997).

then to the extent permitted by this title, payment shall, notwithstanding such determination, be made for such items or services . . . as though section 1862 (a) (1) and section 1862 (a) (9) did not apply.

Once "waiver of liability" applies, the relevant inquiry focuses on whether the provider or supplier knew or could have been reasonably expected to know that payment would not be made for the items or services.[10] If the provider or supplier had actual or constructive notice that services were excluded from coverage as not medically necessary, "waiver of liability" will not apply. Evidence that a provider or supplier knew, or should have known, that payment would not be made for items or services includes the following:

- A Medicare contractor's prior written notice to the specific provider or supplier that it would not provide payment for an item or service (including notice from a Quality Improvement Organization (QIO) or MAC).
- A Medicare contractor's prior written notice to the medical community (e.g., manual instructions, bulletins, the Medicare contractor's written guidelines, etc.) that it would not provide payment for items or services. This means that providers and suppliers are deemed to have knowledge of all provisions of the Medicare Internet-Only Manuals (available at http://www.cms.gov/manuals), articles, bulletins, as well as information maintained on the Medicare contractors' websites.
- Where the items or services rendered were inconsistent with acceptable standards of practice in the local medical community. In determining "acceptable standards of practice" in a local medical community, Medicare contractors rely on published medical literature (generally, scientific data or

---

10. *See* MCPM, *supra* note 8, Ch. 30, section 20.

research studies published in peer-reviewed medical journals or specialty journals), a consensus of expert medical opinion, consultations with medical staff, medical associations and societies and other health experts.[11]

If a provider or supplier provides a beneficiary with proper written advance notice that Medicare likely would deny payment, the beneficiary will be deemed liable for any items or services denied. This notice is proof that both the provider or supplier *and* beneficiary had prior knowledge that Medicare payment would be denied. In these situations, the beneficiary (rather than the provider or supplier) is held liable for any overpayment.[12]

Medicare providers and suppliers face significant challenges when arguing payment should be made under the doctrine of "waiver of liability,"[13] because CMS has taken the position that providers and suppliers are deemed to have knowledge of all materials Medicare contractors publish. However, in those situations where a Medicare contractor is silent as to coverage of certain denied items or services, and/or in those situations where Medicare guidelines are unclear or contradictory, and where the items or services at issue were provided consistent with acceptable standards of practice in the local medical community, health care providers or suppliers should raise the legal theory of "waiver of liability" to contest a claim denial.

---

11. *See* 42 C.F.R. § 411.406, MCPM, *supra* note 8, Ch. 30, section 30.2, and HCFA Ruling 95-1.

12. *See* MCPM, *supra* note 8, Ch. 30, section 30.1.

13. *See, e.g.,* Almy v. Sebelius, 749 F. Supp. 2d 315 (D. Md. 2010), *affirmed* 679 F.3d 297 (finding that a supplier knew or should have known that Medicare coverage would be denied where Medicare contractors had denied several of the supplier's early-filed claims and the supplier had submitted written advance beneficiary notices (ABNs) to its beneficiaries). *See also* Willowood of Great Barrington, Inc. v. Sebelius, 638 F. Supp. 2d 98 (D. Mass., 2009) (finding that "waiver of liability" did not apply, where CMS had published guidance—including manual provisions, NCD, and LCD—related to the services at issue).

D. Provider without Fault

Once a Medicare contractor has concluded that an overpayment exists (i.e., after the Medicare contractor determines that payment cannot be made under the "waiver of liability" provisions of the statute, implementing regulations, and policy), the Medicare contractor next determines whether the provider, the supplier, or the beneficiary was without fault with respect to the overpayment.

The statutory authority for the legal doctrine of "provider without fault" is set forth in Section 1870 of the Social Security Act[14] and states the following:

(a) Any payment under this title to any provider of services or other person with respect to any items or services furnished to an individual shall be regarded as payment to such individual.

(b) Where—

(1) more than the correct amount is paid under this title to a provider of services . . . and the Secretary determines (A) that, within such period as he may specify, the excess over the correct amount cannot be recouped from such provider of services or other person, or (B) that such provider of services . . . was without fault with respect to the payment of such excess over the correct amount . . .

(2) . . . proper adjustments shall be made . . . by decreasing subsequent payments. . . .

(3) to which such individual is entitled . . .

For purposes of clause (B) paragraph (1), such provider of services or such other person shall, in the absence of evidence to the contrary, be deemed to be without fault if the Secretary's determination that more than such correct

---

14. 42 U.S.C. § 1395gg (January 2, 2013).

amount was paid was made subsequent to the fifth year[15] following the year in which notice was sent to such individual that such amount had been paid . . .

(c) There shall be no adjustment provided in subsection (b) (nor shall there be recovery) in any case where the incorrect payments have been made . . . with respect to an individual who is without fault or where the adjustment (or recovery) . . . would be against equity and good conscience. Adjustment or recovery of an incorrect payment . . . against an individual who is without fault shall be deemed to be against equity and good conscience if . . . the Secretary's determination that such payment was incorrect was made subsequent to the fifth year[16] following the year in which notice of such payment was sent to such individual; except that the Secretary may reduce such five-year period to not less than one year if he finds such reduction is consistent with the objectives of this title.

As a general rule (1) a provider or supplier will be without fault if it exercised reasonable care in billing for and accepting payment; (2) and will be *deemed to be* without fault if an overpayment is identified subsequent to the fifth calendar year after the year of payment. If a provider or supplier is without fault with respect to an overpayment, or deemed to be without fault, then liability for the overpayment shifts to the beneficiary.[17]

---

15. Before January 2, 2013, the statute deemed a provider or supplier to be without fault if the Secretary determined that a provider or supplier had been overpaid subsequent to the *third* year following the year in which the provider or supplier initially received notice that the claim would be paid. Pursuant to Section 638 of the American Taxpayer Relief Act of 2012 (Pub. L. No. 112–240, 2012 HR 8), approved January 2, 2013, the three-year time period was increased to five years.
16. *Id.*
17. MEDICARE FINANCIAL MANAGEMENT MANUAL (CMS Internet-Only Publication 100-06) (MFMM), Ch. 3, sections 70.3 and 80, *available at* https://www.cms.gov/Regulations-and-Guidance/Guidance/Manuals/Downloads/fin106c03.pdf.

A provider or supplier will be without fault if it complied with all pertinent regulations, made full disclosure of all material facts, and on the basis of the information available (including all Medicare publications), had a reasonable basis for assuming that the payment was correct.[18] *Fault*, for purposes of the provider without fault provision of the Social Security Act, is defined by the federal regulations as follows:

(a) An incorrect statement made by the individual which he knew or should have known to be incorrect; or
(b) Failure to furnish information which he knew or should have known to be material; or
(c) With respect to the overpaid individual only, acceptance of a payment, which he knew or could have been expected to know, was incorrect.[19]

In addition, providers and suppliers will be deemed to be without fault if an overpayment is discovered subsequent to the fifth calendar year after the year in which payment is made, in the absence of evidence to the contrary. At least one federal court explicitly found that the statute creates a rebuttable presumption of no-fault on the part of the provider if the overpayment is identified after the time frame established by statute (i.e., presently five years).[20] However, it should be noted that this presumption may be overcome if a reviewer determines there is "evidence to the contrary" rebutting the presumption of non-fault.[21]

---

18. *Id.* at section 90.
19. 20 C.F.R. § 404.507.
20. *See, e.g.*, Mt. Sinai Hospital of Greater Miami, Inc. v. Weinberger, 517 F.2d 329, 342 (5th Cir. 1975) (finding that the statute establishes a presumption of non-fault three years following the year in which payment was initially made).
21. *See, e.g., In the case of Holy Cross Hospital v. First Coast Service Options* (Medicare Appeals Council, decided May 13, 2009) (declining to find a provider to be without fault under Section 1870 of the Social Security Act, despite the "rebuttable presumption that providers/suppliers are 'without fault' with regard

The *Medicare Financial Management Manual*, Chapter 3, section 80, summarizes the presumption that a provider or supplier will be deemed to be without fault as follows:

> There are special rules that apply when an overpayment is discovered subsequent to the fifth year following the year in which notice was sent that the amount was paid. Ordinarily, the provider or beneficiary will be considered without fault unless there is evidence to the contrary. In the absence of evidence to the contrary, the FI or carrier will not recover the determined overpayment. (One example of evidence to the contrary would be a pattern of billing errors. *See* Medicare Program Integrity Manual, Publication (PIM) 100-08, Chapter 3.)

Further, for the purposes of determining the time period outside of which a provider or supplier will be deemed to be without fault, the *Medicare Financial Management Manual*, Chapter 3, section 80.1, states the following:

> Only the year of the payment and the year it was found to be an overpayment enter into the determination of the 5-calendar year period. The day and the month are irrelevant. With respect to payments made in 2016, the fifth calendar year thereafter is 2021. For payments made in 2017, the fifth calendar year thereafter is 2022, etc. Thus, the rules apply to payments made in 2016 and discovered to be overpayments after 2021, to payments made in 2017 and discovered to be overpayments after 2022, etc.

---

to overpayments discovered more than three calendar years after the year on which the initial determination was made," in a case where the Council concluded there was evidence contrary to the presumption that the provider was without fault where published manual provisions were not satisfied).

In situations where providers and suppliers have received information from a Medicare contractor confirming the appropriateness of billing the items or services at issue; where providers and suppliers have complied with pertinent Medicare publications (such as NCDs, LCDs, manual provisions, articles and/or bulletins); and/or where an overpayment is identified subsequent to the fifth calendar year following the year in which the provider or supplier received notice that the claim was initially paid, "provider without fault" applies.[22]

E. Challenges to Statistical Extrapolations

In many post-payment audits, a CMS contractor will audit a small sample of a provider's or supplier's records. If it finds an overpayment, the contractor will extrapolate the overpayment to a defined universe.[23] As noted in Chapter 2, MACs, SMRCs, RACs, and UPICs all are authorized to use statistical sampling and extrapolation to estimate an overpayment.

1. Medicare Prescription Drug, Improvement and Modernization Act

The Medicare Prescription Drug, Improvement and Modernization Act (MMA) places limits on a Medicare contractor's use of statistical extrapolation. Although Medicare contractors are granted

---

22. *See, e.g., In the case of Comprehensive Decubitus Therapy, Inc., d/b/a Advanced Tissue v. CIGNA* (DME MAC), decided March 13, 2009 (finding a provider "without fault" with respect to an overpayment); *but see* NOR Community Mental Health Corp. v. HHS, 2011 WL 91982 (D. Puerto Rico) (in which the court applied Provider without Fault (Section 1870), and found that the provider was not without fault where it did not comply with a published Local Medical Review Policy).

23 *See* Jessica L. Gustafson, Esq. and Abby Pendleton, Esq., CMS REVISES GUIDANCE REGARDING THE USE OF STATISTICAL SAMPLING FOR OVERPAYMENT ESTIMATION, ABA HEALTH eSOURCE, Vol. 15, No. 11, July 1, 2019.

wide latitude in designing and performing statistical studies, this leeway is not totally unencumbered.

Pursuant to Section 935 of the MMA (Section 1893(f)(3) of the Social Security Act[24]):

> (1) LIMITATION ON USE OF EXTRAPOLATION—A Medicare contractor may not use extrapolation to determine overpayment amounts to be recovered by recoupment, offset, or otherwise, unless the Secretary determines that—
>> (A) There is a sustained or high level of payment error; or
>> (B) Documented educational intervention has failed to correct the error.
>
> There shall be no administrative or judicial review under section 1869, section 1878, or otherwise, of determinations by the Secretary of sustained or high levels of payment errors under this paragraph.[25]

Although the MMA provides that there shall be no administrative or judicial review of determinations made by the Secretary of a sustained or high level of payment errors, an argument exists that the statute does not preclude judicial or administrative review of a decision to use statistical extrapolation to estimate an overpayment when the requisite determination of a high level of payment error or lack of documented educational intervention has not occurred in the first instance.[26]

---

24. 42 U.S.C. § 1395ddd(f)(3) (December 8, 2003).

25. *See also* 42 C.F.R. § 405.926(p) and MEDICARE PROGRAM INTEGRITY MANUAL (CMS Pub. 100-08) (MPIM), Ch. 8, section 8.4.1.2.

26. The Council has considered this argument, with varied outcome: *See In the Case of Cabarrus Podiatry Clinic* (decided December 14, 2007), which found that where neither CMS nor the contractor made the requisite determination pursuant to Section 1893(f)(3) of the Social Security Act, the ALJ was entitled to disregard the projection. *But see also In the case of John Shimko, DPM d/b/a Lakeside Foot Clinic v. Cigna Government Services* (decided October 15, 2009), finding that neither the Council nor the underlying ALJ had jurisdiction

The MPIM, Chapter 8, section 8.4.1.4, describes when a Medicare contractor *shall* and *may* use statistical sampling and extrapolation. In particular, this section of the MPIM provides that a contractor *shall* use statistical sampling when the criteria set forth in Section 935 of the MMA are satisfied—i.e., "when it has been determined that a sustained or high level of payment error exists." The MPIM specifies that sustained or high level of payment error shall be determined to exist in a multitude of scenarios, including but not limited to the following:

- The contractor (or other medical review) identifies an error rate greater than or equal to 50 percent;
- The provider or supplier has a history of non-compliance for the same or similar issue;
- CMS may approve the use of statistical sampling in connection with a payment suspension;
- The contractor obtains information of payment errors via law enforcement investigations;
- Current or former employee(s) of the provider or supplier alleges that the provider or supplier has engaged in wrongdoing;
- The Department of Health and Human Services' Office of Inspector General (OIG) identifies a sustained or high level of payment error during an audit or evaluation; and
- Data analysis.[27]

On the other hand, statistical sampling and extrapolation *may* be used "after documented educational intervention failed to cor-

---

to review the Secretary's decision to undertake statistical sampling. *See* MPIM, *supra* note 25, Ch. 8, section 8.4.1.4.

27. If a contractor identifies an overpayment solely based on data analysis, it must consult with its Contracting Officer's Representative (COR) Business Function Lead (BFL) regarding the alleged overpayment. It must also consult with its COR BFL on whether statistical sampling and extrapolation are necessary to identify the alleged overpayment. *See* MPIM *supra* note 25, Ch. 8, section 8.4.1.4.

rect the payment error,"—e.g., if the provider or supplier does not demonstrate adequate improvement through the Targeted Probe and Educate (TPE) process (outlined in Chapter 2 of this book).[28]

2. Challenges to the Validity of a Statistical Sample

HCFA Ruling 86-1 established Medicare's formal policy on its contractors' use of statistical sampling and extrapolation to estimate overpayments. HCFA Ruling 86-1 "held that the use of statistical sampling to project an overpayment is consistent with the Government's common law right to recover overpayments, the Medicare statute, and the Department's regulations, and does not deny a provider or supplier due process."[29] Although HCFA Ruling 86-1 allows Medicare contractors to use statistical sampling to estimate overpayments, the Ruling clarifies that providers and suppliers are afforded due process rights to appeal the validity of a statistical sample and the resulting overpayment. Specifically, pursuant to HCFA Ruling 86-1:

> Sampling does not deprive a provider of its right to challenge the sample, nor of its rights to procedural due process.[30] Sampling only creates a presumption of validity as to the amount of an overpayment which may be used as the basis for recoupment. The burden then shifts to the provider to take the next step. *The provider could attack the statistical validity of the sample, or it could challenge the correctness of the determination in specific cases identified by the sample (including waiver of liability where medical*

---

28. *Id.*

29. HCFA Ruling 86-1 at 14.

30. In the landmark case of *Chaves County Home Health Service, Inc. v. Sullivan,* the court found that statistical sampling does not violate an appellant's procedural due process rights, "so long as the extrapolation is made from a representative sample and is statistically significant." Chaves County Home Health Service, Inc. v. Sullivan, 931 F.2d 914 (D.C. Cir. 1991), *cert. denied,* 402 U.S. 1091 (1992).

necessity or custodial care is at issue).[31] In either case, the provider is given a full opportunity to demonstrate that the overpayment determination is wrong. If certain individual cases within the sample are determined to be decided erroneously, the amount of overpayment projected to the universe of claims can be modified. If the statistical basis upon which the projection was based is successfully challenged, the overpayment determination can be corrected.

Chapter 8, section 8.4 of the MPIM provides instructions to Medicare contractors on their use of statistical sampling and extrapolation for overpayment estimation. Contractors are afforded significant flexibility to design statistical samples for the purpose of estimating overpayments. However, regardless of the process of sample selection employed, CMS requires that it result in a "probability sample." Pursuant to the MPIM, Chapter 8, section 8.4.2:

> For a procedure to be classified as probability sampling, the following two features must apply:
>
> - It must be possible, in principle, to enumerate a set of distinct samples that the procedure is capable of selecting if applied to the target universe. Although only one sample will be selected, each distinct sample of the set has a known probability of selection . . .
> - Each sampling unit in each distinct possible sample must have a known probability of selection. In the case of statistical sampling for overpayment estimation, one of the possible samples is selected by a random process according to which each sampling unit in the target population

---

31. Emphasis added. Pursuant to 42 C.F.R. § 405.1064, "When an appeal from the QIC involves an overpayment issue and the QIC used a statistical sample in reaching its reconsideration, the ALJ must base his or her decision on a review of the entire statistical sample used by the QIC."

receives its appropriate chance of selection. The selection probabilities do not have to be equal, but they should all be greater than zero . . . [32]

Further, "If a particular probability sample is properly executed, i.e., defining the universe, the frame, the sampling units, using proper randomization, accurately measuring the variables of interest, and using the correct formulas for estimation, then assertions that the same or that the resulting estimates are 'not statistically valid' cannot legitimately be made. In other words, a probability sample and its results are always valid."[33]

---

32. *See* MPIM, *supra* note 25, section 8.4.2.

33. *Id.* MPIM, *supra* note 25, section 8.4.1.3 sets for the Steps for Conducting Statistical Sampling, including:

The major steps in conducting statistical sampling are –

(1) Identifying the provider/supplier;

(2) Identifying the period to be reviewed;

(3) Defining the universe (target population) and the sampling unit, and constructing the sampling frame;

(4) Assessing the distribution of the paid amounts in the sample frame to determine the sample design; it is very likely that the distribution of the overpayments will not be normal. However, there are many sampling methodologies (for example, use of the Central Limit Theorem) that may be used to accommodate non-normal distributions. The statistician should state the assumptions being made about the distribution and explain the sampling methodology selected as a result of that distribution.

(5) Performing the appropriate assessment(s) to determine whether the sample size is appropriate for the statistical analyses used, and identifying, relative to the sample size used, the corresponding confidence interval;

(6) Designing the sampling plan and selecting the sample from the sampling frame;

(7) Examining each of the sampling units and determining if there was an overpayment or an underpayment; and

Frustratingly for provider and supplier appellants, CMS does not require that its contractors comply with all aspects of the guidelines set forth in the MPIM. As noted by the MPIM, Chapter 8, section 8.4.1.4, "Failure by a contractor to follow one or more of the requirements contained herein does not necessarily affect the validity of the statistical sampling that was conducted or the projection of the overpayment. . . . Failure by a contractor to follow one or more of the requirements contained herein may result in review by CMS of their performance, but should not be construed as necessarily affecting the validity of the statistical sampling and/or the projection of the overpayment."[34] Thus, for an

---

(8) Estimating the overpayment.

When an overpayment has been determined to exist, the contractor shall follow applicable instructions for notification and collection of the overpayment, unless otherwise directed by CMS. For each step, the contractor shall provide complete and clear documentation sufficient to explain the action(s) taken in the step and to replicate, if needed, the statistical sampling.

34. *See e.g., In the case of San Bois Health Services, Inc* (decided October 30, 2014), finding, "Suffice it to say that, given the MPIM provisions, the fact that a contractor may have selected sample claims by a process that another statistician may not prefer, does not provide a basis for invalidating the sampling or the extrapolation as actually drawn and conducted." In this case, the Council overturned the ALJ's finding that the statistics were invalid, when the appellant presented expert testimony, the ALJ called an independent statistical expert who presented testimony, and the ZPIC's statistician did not participate in the ALJ hearing. *See also, e.g., In the case of Maxxim Care, EMS v. Trailblazer Health Enterprises, LLC* (decided February 25, 2010), which finds, "Thus, the provisions of CMS Ruling 86-1 establish that the burden is on the appellant to prove that the statistical sampling methodology was invalid, and not on the contractor to establish that it chose the most precise methodology." *See also, e.g.,* Maxxim Care EMS v Sebelius, 2011 WL 5977666 (S.D. Tax, Nov. 29, 2011) (upholding the Council decision referenced above). *See also, e.g., In the case of Transyd Enterprises, LLC d/b/a Transpro Medical Transport v. TrailBlazer Health Enterprises, LLC* (decided September 15, 2009), which states, "[T]he burden is on the appellant to prove that the statistical sampling methodology was invalid, and not on the contractor to establish that it chose the most precise methodol-

appellant to successfully challenge the validity of a statistical sample and extrapolation, it must go beyond identifying the portions of the MPIM with which the CMS contractor failed to comply. The appellant must establish that the CMS contractor failed to properly execute its chosen sample design to such extent that it did not result in a probability sample, and that, accordingly, the validity of the sample and extrapolation were nullified.[35]

Increasingly, after an ALJ has issued a decision ruling a statistical sample to be invalid, CMS has decided, on its "own motion," to review the ALJ's decision—alleging that it contained an error of law material to the outcome of the claims and/or alleging that the decision is not supported by the preponderance of the evidence.[36]

---

ogy." *See also, e.g.*, Pruchniewski v. Leavitt, 2006 WL 2331071 (M.D. Fla. Aug. 10, 2006), finding that "under Ruling 86-1, sampling creates a presumption of validity as to the amount of overpayment and the burden of attacking the statistical validity of the sample is shifted to the provider."

35. *See In the case of John Sanders, M.D. v. CIGNA Government Services* (decided May 12, 2011), which found that the execution of the sampling conducted was substantively flawed, and therefore, the overpayment was limited to the actual sampled claims without extrapolation.

36. *See* 42 C.F.R. §§ 405.1110, which states:

(a) *General rule.* The Council may decide on its own motion to review a decision or dismissal issued by an ALJ or attorney adjudicator. CMS or any of its contractors may refer a case to the Council for it to consider reviewing under this authority anytime within 60 calendar days after the date of an ALJ's or attorney adjudicator's decision or dismissal.

(b) *Referral of cases.* (1) CMS or any of its contractors may refer a case to the Council if, in their view, the decision or dismissal contains an error of law material to the outcome of the claim or presents a broad policy or procedural issue that may affect the public interest. CMS may also request that the Council take own motion review of a case if—

(i) CMS or its contractor participated in the appeal at the OMHA level; and

(ii) In CMS' view, the ALJ's or attorney adjudicator's decision or dismissal is not supported by the preponderance of evidence in the record or the ALJ or attorney adjudicator abused his or her discretion...

Acknowledging the flexibility within the MPIM, Council decisions often overrule ALJ decisions that rule a statistical sample and corresponding projection to be invalid.[37]

Relying on language within the MPIM cited above that "Failure by a contractor to follow one or more of the requirements . . . should not be construed as necessarily affecting the validity of the statistical sampling and/or the projection of the overpayment,"[38] the Council's position seems to be that there are few, if any, errors or omissions that a contractor could make in performing a statistical sample and projection that would be significant enough to invalidate a contractor's sample and projection to estimate an overpayment. In other words, if the contractor produces enough information to describe the process followed by the contractor in conducting its sample and projection, the Council has demonstrated reluctance to find the process invalid, even when confronted by the opinions of experts in the field of statistics to the contrary.[39]

Despite the high bar set by the Council for a provider or supplier to successfully challenge the validity of the sample and a

---

37. *See e.g.,* Overpayment Claims, *available at* https://www.hhs.gov/about/agencies/dab/decisions/council-decisions/index.html.

38. *See,* Section 8.4.1.4—Determining When Statistical Sampling May Be Used, Change Request 10067, Transmittal 828 (September 28, 2018), *available at* https://www.cms.gov/Regulations-and-Guidance/Guidance/Transmittals/2018 Downloads/R828PI.pdf.

39. *See, e.g.: In the case of Sans Bois Health Services, Inc.,* Docket Number M-14-2629 (Decided October 30, 2014); *In the case of Anthony Pagliarulo, M.D.,* Docket Number M-14-2132 (decided September 26, 2014); and *In the case of Robert D. Lesser, M.D. & Associates,* Docket Number M-11-2354 (decided December 7, 2011), all *available at* https://www.hhs.gov/about/agencies/dab/decisions/council-decisions/index.html.

In *Maxmed Healthcare Inc. v. Burwell,* 152 F.Supp.3d 639 (W.D. Tex. 2016), the federal district court for the Western District of Texas upheld the Council's analysis finding a statistical sample and projection to be valid after the ALJ found it to be invalid, and the Council reversed. In *Maxmed,* the court noted that it must give "substantial deference to the [Council's] interpretation." Maxmed Healthcare Inc. v. Burwell, 152 F.Supp.3d 619 at 625 (WD Tex. 2016) (citing Girling Health Care v. Shalala, 85 F.3d 211 at 215 (5th Cir. 1996)).

corresponding projection to estimate an overpayment, attorneys representing providers and suppliers appealing an extrapolated overpayment determination should exercise their procedural due process rights to challenge the validity of the sample and corresponding projection.

a. Request Copies of the Entire Contractor Case File

The MPIM requires Medicare contractors to maintain documentation to allow another to recreate the sample frame and sample, including information regarding the sampling methodology followed.[40] The contractor also must maintain documentation to allow an overpayment calculation to be replicated and validated.[41] When the contractor provides such information to an appellant, such information is invaluable to the statistical expert retained to assist with the appeal. If the contractor fails to provide such information or if there are discrepancies within it, the Council has used this failure to maintain and provide appropriate documentation to an appellant as a basis to not uphold a statistical projection. For example:

- *In the case of Podiatric Medical Associates,* Docket Number M-10-230 (decided June 22, 2010), the Council found:

  > It is well-established that due process affords an appellant provider the right to examine audit results in order to mount a proper challenge in the appeals process. Not only was pertinent audit-related information withheld from the appellant, the inaccessibility of the CDs in the record forwarded to the Council by the ALJ leads to the conclusion that the record upon which the ALJ relied in upholding audit extrapolation was incomplete. An ALJ decision must be based on

---

40. MPIM *supra* note 25, Ch. 8, § 8.4.3.2 and § 8.4.4.4.
41. *Id.* at § 8.4.4.5.

evidence offered at the hearing or otherwise admitted into the record. 42 C.F.R. § 405.1046(a). Absent supporting evidence, the appellant is deprived of its ability to review the extrapolation in question.

For these reasons, the Council reverses the extrapolation of the audit results at issue here.[42]

- *In the case of Global Home Care,* Docket Number M-11-116 (decided January 11, 2011), the Council found:

  The record in this case does not contain complete documentation to support the use of statistical sampling and extrapolation to calculate Medicare's overpayment to the appellant. The sampling frame cannot be recreated from the documentation present. Without this basic documentation, a provider does not have the information and data necessary to mount a due process challenge to the statistical validity of the sample, as is its right under CMS Ruling 86-1.[43]

- *In the case of John Sanders, M.D.,* Docket Number M-11-869 (decided May 12, 2011), the Council found:

  [T]here were two sampling issues raised by the appellant, which were neither sufficiently explained nor corrected by the [contractor], and which were the subject of testimony from the independent expert statistician. These two errors are not addressed in or rebutted by the CMS memorandum. The errors are: 1) the [contractor] provided the independent statistical expert with sample data which assigned some claims to the

---

42. *In the case of Podiatric Medical Associates,* Docket Number M-10-230 (decided June 22, 2010).
43. *In the case of Global Home Care,* Docket Number M-11-116 (decided January 11, 2011).

wrong stratum; and 2) the [contractor] provided the independent expert with a second CD containing an Excel set of sample data with significant discrepancies from the first set of data, and the [contractor] was unable to clarify the discrepancies, to identify which set of data was applicable, or to explain the significance of the second set of data. The Council finds that these errors and inconsistencies in the original sampling preclude use of the sample to extrapolate an overpayment to the full universe of claims.[44]

b. Engage an Expert in Statistics

When a Medicare contractor chooses to use a statistical sample and projection to estimate an overpayment, the MPIM, Chapter 8, section 8.1.4.5 requires the sampling methodology to be reviewed and approved by a statistician (or person with equivalent experience in probability sampling and estimation). A contractor's statistician must meet the following educational and professional qualifications:

- Have significant coursework in probability and estimation methodologies, and at least 10 years of experience applying methods of statistical sampling and interpreting the results.
- Possess a Bachelor's degree (e.g., B.A., B.S.) in statistics or in some related field (e.g., psychometrics, biostatistics, econometrics, mathematics) with significant coursework in probability and estimation methodologies and at least six years of experience applying methods of statistical sampling and interpreting the results.
- Possess a Master's degree (e.g., M.A., M.S.) in statistics or in some related field with significant coursework in proba-

---

44. *In the case of John Sanders, M.D.,* Docket Number M-11-869 (decided May 12, 2011). *But see also In the case of Anthony Pagliarulo, M.D.,* Docket Number M-14-2132 (decided September 26, 2014), finding that, even where multiple universe files were supplied, the statistical sample and projection were valid.

bility and estimation methodologies and at least four years of experience applying methods of statistical sampling and interpreting the results.

- Possess a Doctoral degree in statistics or in some related field with significant coursework in probability and estimation methodologies and at least one year of experience applying methods of statistical sampling and interpreting the results.[45]

In challenging the validity of a statistical sample and projection to estimate an overpayment, it is essential to engage a qualified expert to review the contractor's case file and opine regarding the validity of the statistical sample and projection. The appellant's expert statistician should satisfy the educational and professional qualifications required of the contractor's statistician. An adjudicator's determination as to whether a statistical sample and projection is valid is based on a comparison of the experts' testimonies.[46] The appellant's expert statistician should prepare a written report analyzing the validity of the sample and projection, which should be submitted as soon as possible in the appeals process (as, at times, a statistical sample and projection may be found to be invalid at stages in the appeals process prior to the ALJ stage of appeal). It is also important that the appellant's expert statistician is able to explain to the ALJ, in lay terms, the rationale for his or her findings, should the appeal proceed to the ALJ stage of appeal.

---

45. *See* Section 8.4.1.5
46. *See e.g., Maxmed Healthcare Inc.* 152 F.Supp.3d 639, which found that the appellant's expert witness conclusion that the sampling units were not independent was not supported because, "only one of the three expert witnesses opined that the sampling units are, in fact, dependent."

Resources and Reference Materials

The following resources may assist health care attorneys representing providers and suppliers subject to post-payment or pre-payment claims reviews and audits. The resources and references listed below constitute a sampling of available resources; more specific citations are included within the body of Chapters 1, 2, and 3.

A. ABA Health Law Section Resources

- *The Health Lawyer*—The American Bar Association (ABA) Health Law Section publishes *The Health Lawyer* on a bimonthly basis. The in-depth articles included within this publication focus on an array of health law topics. Articles are prepared by ABA Health Law Section members and edited by the magazine's editorial board. Information related to *The Health Lawyer* (including past issues) is available at http://www.americanbar.org/publications/health_lawyer_home.html.
- *ABA Health eSource*—The ABA Health Law Section also publishes a monthly electronic newsletter distributed to ABA Health Law Section members. Information related to the *ABA Health eSource* (including past issues) is available at http://www.americanbar.org/content/newsletter/publications/aba_health_esource_home.html.
- Daniel A. Cody and Kathleen Scully-Hayes, *A Practical Guide to Medicare Appeals* (Chicago: American Bar Association, 2007).

- David Daniel Mullens, *How to Win Medicare Appeals* (Chicago: American Bar Association, 2020).

B. Government Resources

- Centers for Medicare & Medicaid Services (CMS) home page: http://www.cms.gov.
- CMS Original Medicare (i.e., Fee-for-service) Appeals webpage: http://www.cms.gov/Medicare/Appeals-and-Grievances/OrgMedFFSAppeals/index.html?redirect=/OrgMedFFSAppeals/.
- Office of the Inspector General of HHS home page: http://www.oig.hhs.gov.
- CMS Comprehensive Error Rate Testing (CERT) program webpage: http://www.cms.gov/CERT.
- CMS Supplemental Medical Review Contractor (SMRC) program webpage: http://www.cms.gov/Research-Statistics-Data-and-Systems/Monitoring-Programs/Medicare-FFS-Compliance-Programs/Medical-Review/SMRC.html.
- CMS Recovery Audit webpage: http://www.cms.gov/Research-Statistics-Data-and-Systems/Monitoring-Programs/Medicare-FFS-Compliance-Programs/Recovery-Audit-Program/.
- CMS Center for Program Integrity webpage: http://www.cms.gov/About-CMS/Components/CPI/Center-for-program-integrity.html.

C. Statutory, Regulatory (i.e., Code of Federal Regulations ("[CFR]")), and Sub-Regulatory Guidance Citations Related to the Medicare Part A and Part B FFS Appeals Process and Medicare Audits

- Section 1869 of the Social Security Act (42 U.S.C. § 1395ff)—This portion of the Social Security Act sets forth the Medicare Part A and Part B FFS appeals process.

- 42 C.F.R. Part 405 Subpart I—This portion of the CFR codifies Section 1869 of the Social Security Act.
- *Medicare Claims Processing Manual* (MCPM) (CMS Internet-Only Publication 100-04), Chapter 29—This chapter of the MCPM provides detailed guidance regarding the Medicare Part A and Part B FFS appeals process.
- *Medicare Program Integrity Manual* (MPIM) (CMS Internet-Only Publication 100-08), Chapter 1—This chapter of the MPIM provides an overview of medical review and benefit integrity audits.
- MPIM, Chapter 3—This chapter provides detailed information regarding post-payment and pre-payment review programs.
- MPIM, Chapter 4—This chapter describes the CMS benefit integrity review process.

D. Statutory, Regulatory, and Sub-Regulatory Guidance Citations Related to the Medicare Part A and Part B FFS Related to Legal Challenges to Medicare Audit Determinations

1. Treating Physician Rule

- Section 1862(a) of the Social Security Act (42 U.S.C § 1395y)—Pursuant to Section 1862(a) of the Social Security Act (42 U.S.C § 1395y), payment may not be made under Medicare Part A or Part B for items or services that "are not reasonable and necessary for the diagnosis or treatment of illness or injury or to improve the functioning of a malformed body member."
- Section 1801 of the Social Security Act (42 U.S.C. § 1395)—This portion of the Social Security Act sets forth the foundation for the "treating physician rule."
- HCFA Ruling 93-1—HCFA Ruling 93-1 sets forth CMS's position related to the applicability of the "treating physician rule."

2. Waiver of Liability

- Section 1862(a) of the Social Security Act (42 U.S.C § 1395y)—Pursuant to Section 1862(a) of the Social Security Act (42 U.S.C § 1395y), payment may not be made under Medicare Part A or Part B for items or services that "are not reasonable and necessary for the diagnosis or treatment of illness or injury or to improve the functioning of a malformed body member."
- Section 1879 of the Social Security Act (42 U.S.C. § 1395pp)—This section of the Social Security Act sets forth the Waiver of Liability provisions of law.
- 42 C.F.R. § 411.406—This federal regulation sets forth the criteria to be applied to determine whether a provider or supplier knew that items or services would be excluded from coverage as not medically necessary.
- *Medicare Financial Management Manual*, Chapter 3, section 70.1—This portion of the MFMM provides guidance related to the Waiver of Liability portions of the Social Security Act.
- MCPM, Ch. 30, sections 30 through 30.2.3—Chapter 30 of the MCPM sets forth guidance related to the financial liability protections of the Social Security Act.
- HCFA Ruling 95-1—HCFA Ruling 95-1 sets forth the CMS general policy related to determining when the limitation of liability provisions of the Social Security Act apply.

3. Provider without Fault

- Section 1870 of the Social Security Act (42 U.S.C. § 1395gg)—Section 1870 of the Social Security Act sets forth the Provider without Fault provisions of law.
- 20 C.F.R. § 404.507—This federal regulation defines the term *fault* for purposes of the Provider without Fault provisions of law.
- *Medicare Financial Management Manual*, Chapter 3, sections 70.3 through 110.11—This portion of the MFMM

provides guidance related to the Provider without Fault portions of the Social Security Act.

- Department Appeals Board, Medicare Appeals Council decisions related to fault are available at http://www.hhs.gov/dab/divisions/medicareoperations/macdecisions/mac_decisions.html#overpayment_claims.

4. Challenges to Statistical Extrapolations

- Section 935 of the MMA (Section 1893(f)(3) of the Social Security Act (42 U.S.C. § 1395ddd(f)(3))—This portion of the MMA creates limitations on a contractor's use of extrapolation.
- MPIM, Chapter 8—Chapter 8 of the MPIM provides guidance to contractors in performing audits involving statistical samples and extrapolation.
- HCFA Ruling 86-1—HCFA Ruling 86-1 sets forth the CMS general policy regarding the use of statistical sampling and extrapolation and includes cites to numerous authorities for this position.
- Department Appeals Board, Medicare Appeals Council decisions related to statistical extrapolations are available at http://www.hhs.gov/dab/divisions/medicareoperations/mac decisions/mac_decisions.html#overpayment_claims.

Index

Note: Page numbers with n indicate footnotes.

appointment of representative
(AOR), 27–28
automated review, 17

B
backlog and resolution, 35–36
beneficiary's liability for
overpayment, 50, 52
Business Function Lead (BFL),
57n27

C
*Cabarrus Podiatry Clinic, In the
case of,* 56n26
carriers, 6–7, 20
Center for Program Integrity
(CPI), 2, 21, 70
Centers for Medicare &
Medicaid Services (CMS)
Medicare auditing
initiatives, 1–25
Medicare Part A and Part B
appeals process, 27–41
Medicare Part A and Part B
audit determinations,
43–67
resources and reference
materials, 70–73
Chair of the Department Appeals
Board (DAB), 44
*Chaves County Home Health
Service, Inc. v. Sullivan,*
58n30
claim reviews, 17–18
Code of Federal Regulations
(CFR), 9, 70–71
coding reviews, 17, 18, 23, 24, 44

Cody, Daniel A., 69
complex review, 17–18, 24
*Comprehensive Decubitus
Therapy, Inc., d/b/a Advanced
Tissue v. CIGNA,* 55n22
Comprehensive Error Rate
Testing (CERT) audits, 1, 2–6
appeals process, 6
error rate measurement and
estimation process, 4–5
establishment of, 3–4
Medicare FFS error rate,
3–4
purpose of, 1, 3, 5–6
Contracting Officer's
Representative (COR), 57n27
contractor case file, request for
copies of, 64–66
contractor-level error rate, 3–4, 6
COR BFL (Contracting Officer's
Representative Business
Function Lead), 57n27
coverage determinations
Local Coverage
Determinations (LCDs),
7, 18, 32, 34, 55
National Coverage
Determinations (NCDs),
18, 32, 34, 55
responsible parties for, in
MAC audits, 12

D
demand letter, 12–13, 19, 25, 30
Dennis v. Shalala, 46n6
Department Appeals Board
(DAB), 44